"THERE ARE MANY WAYS YOU CAN REACT. . . . YOU WILL BE SHOCKED, NUMB, FRUSTRATED, ANGRY. NO, NOT JUST ANGRY; MAD. MAD AS HELL. FINE. FEEL ANGRY. TOWERING RAGE CAN BE A USEFUL STIMULANT. JUST USE IT, DON'T LET IT USE YOU. GET EVEN BY RISING TO GREATER HEIGHTS THAN WOULD EVER HAVE BEEN POSSIBLE IF YOU STAYED. . . ."

Like so many others, you may have lost your "secure" job in the rampant downsizing of the 1990s—or you may see the handwriting on the wall. Welcome to dangerous times. This sympathetic but no-nonsense book is your survival guide for recovering from job loss, both emotionally and financially, with everything you need to know for jumping back into today's fluctuating job market.

CHRISTOPHER KIRKWOOD has worked in the financial services and health care industries for the past 25 years. He is currently the manager of a large nonprofit corporation. Having changed jobs seven times in the past 20 years, he brings singular firsthand experience to the writing of this book.

YOUR SERVICES ARE NO LONGER REQUIRED
The Complete Job-Loss Recovery Book

Your Services Are No Longer Required

THE COMPLETE JOB-LOSS RECOVERY BOOK

Christopher Kirkwood

A PLUME BOOK

PLUME
Published by the Penguin Group
Penguin Books USA Inc., 375 Hudson Street,
New York, New York 10014, U.S.A.
Penguin Books Ltd, 27 Wrights Lane, London W8 5TZ, England
Penguin Books Australia Ltd, Ringwood, Victoria, Australia
Penguin Books Canada Ltd, 10 Alcorn Avenue,
Toronto, Ontario, Canada M4V 3B2
Penguin Books (N.Z.) Ltd, 182–190 Wairau Road, Auckland 10, New Zealand

Penguin Books Ltd, Registered Offices:
Harmondsworth, Middlesex, England

First published by Plume, an imprint of New American Library,
a division of Penguin Books USA Inc.

First Printing, February, 1993
10 9 8 7 6 5 4 3 2 1

REGISTERED TRADEMARK—MARCA REGISTRADA

LIBRARY OF CONGRESS CATALOGING-IN-PUBLICATION DATA:

Kirkwood, Christopher.
    Your services are no longer required : the complete job-loss
recovery book / Christopher Kirkwood.
        p.   cm.
    Include index.
    ISBN 0-452-26947-4
    1. Employees—Dismissal of. 2. Professional employees—
Psychology. 3. Unemployment. 4. Job hunting. I. Title.
HF5549.5.D55K57   1993
650.14—dc20   92-24375
                                                         CIP

Printed in the United States of America
Set in Caledonia
Designed by Eve L. Kirch

BOOKS ARE AVAILABLE AT QUANTITY DISCOUNTS WHEN USED TO PROMOTE PRODUCTS
OR SERVICES. FOR INFORMATION PLEASE WRITE TO PREMIUM MARKETING DIVISION,
PENGUIN BOOKS USA INC., 375 HUDSON STREET, NEW YORK, NEW YORK 10014.

To Lynn, for so many things

Contents

Introduction

This is a book for people who have lost or think they might lose their jobs and who need help in recovering. It is for women and men, because business today is an equal-opportunity terminator. It is a book for optimists, at a time when it's difficult to be anything but a pessimist. It is for people who want to take personal control of their careers, in an era when the workplace is becoming more impersonal and, seemingly, beyond anyone's control. And it's for people who have begun to understand that to exercise control, they will have to do many things differently. But they aren't sure how to proceed, not certain about what they'll have to do differently or what new commitments they'll have to make to secure their future.

This book is intended to lead you step-by-step toward that future, by sharing with you the experiences and the lessons learned by those who've been through what you are just starting through, or are worried about.

In these pages you'll share, if you haven't yet, the trauma of suddenly losing your job. You'll get a sense of what it's like to be unexpectedly flat on your back, and the feelings you'll experience. Learning to cope with them will be a top priority; so will completing your separation on the most favorable terms. Information on how to keep your finances in shape will be provided, and you'll be steered through a successful launch of your job search.

At the same time, an effort will be made to get you to look back at possible personal mistakes that may have speeded your exit. And you'll be advised on how to cope with the more difficult people you may be working with in the future.

Then we'll shift into high gear and consider how to successfully conclude your job search quickly—a new job in sixty days should be your primary objective; we'll tell you why—and minimize your chances for needing to conduct another search involuntarily. You'll be shown why getting a new job, as important as that is, doesn't or shouldn't complete your recovery.

You will learn what you have to do to attain a real degree of financial independence, and why that's an important part of your recovery. This is not a get-rich-quick scheme, or a plan for making it using someone else's money, but plans and ideas that have worked and still work. All these things require difficult choices; these will be spelled out for you. If you have the fortitude to make the choices and stick to the plans, year after year, there is no way short of a major catastrophe that success in your recovery can be denied you.

Finally, we'll pull all the pieces together, integrating career and financial planning, to help you gain the most satisfying control of your career, and your life. This will mark the completion of the first and most important part of your recovery.

Although we've never met, I know one thing about you: You either have lost your job or you will. This is true no matter what your position or income level, no matter how obscure your job, or how exalted. Involuntary job loss is a fact of life today. Being fired is so common that the word has fallen into disuse. *Outplacement* is what it's now called, and *outplacement counseling* is one of our new growth industries.

As common as it has become, and no matter what it's called, it will still always be one of life's truly traumatic experiences. Anyone who's been through the experience once, or more than once, has learned that. But few people who have been through the experience have learned much else. Far too many people believe that the first time they lose their job will be the last time. They've never had to look hard for a job before, and they've never had to work hard at staying in a job. They've assumed from the beginning of their careers that competence, honesty, hard work, and loyalty were enough.

In the working world of the 1990s they are no longer enough.

Welcome to the world of corporations constantly fine-tuning all their needs, including their needs for people. Welcome to the world of massive cutbacks—as on Wall Street in the last few years and in "white-collar" service industries across the country—and of constant minor layoffs. The term *layoff* is used here interchangeably with *termination,* to connote people who have no expectation of being called back to work, as their companies struggle to stay competitive in the fiercely competitive new world economy. Welcome to dangerous times. They are not going to go away.

Those of you who have never had the experience of a job loss, and even those experiencing it for the first time, may find this impossible to accept, may want to believe that their first experience with outplacement will be their last.

If that's your inclination, you need read no further. But if you're more than a little shaken up by what's happened to you or what you see happening around you, this book will help.

In these pages you will not find a detached, abstract compilation of clichés, theories, and statistics. You will get instead the distillation of the experience of many years in the trenches of corporate America. I have been on both sides of the outplacement cycle. I've had to let people go, and I've left when I didn't want to, and I've moved to new and better jobs when I saw the opportunity.

To benefit from this experience, and the experience of others I've learned from, you'll have to go through the whole cycle, on the way down, climbing back up, finally reaching toward the kind of independence that nobody can take away from you. You will recover and take control of your career, from today until the day you are ready to pack it in—on *your* terms.

If you are reading this soon after being fired or forced to take early retirement, my heart goes out to you. You probably never thought you could feel as lousy as you do now. You may well come to feel a lot worse before you have any reason to feel better. Such feelings are normal, but you won't have the luxury of wallowing in them for long. For this book is about much more than the recovery that is your most immediate concern. It is about taking control of your future. To get there will take hard work, imagination, fortitude, a salesperson's ability to handle rejection, and above all, determination. If you have these qualities, and follow the advice offered here, you will stack the odds in the job market in your favor to a degree you can't imagine now.

Nobody can guarantee you success at anything. What's offered here is realistic hope, by using methods of recovering and controlling your career that have worked for me and for many others. The real expectation of success is the good news that awaits you in this book.

Now let's get to work.

CHAPTER ONE

Being Terminated

This Time It's Different

Changing jobs in the past wasn't nearly the traumatizing experience it has become today. Why? Because not since the Great Depression have so many job losses been *permanent*. There is no nationwide depression that is putting millions of people out of work everywhere. As a matter of fact, the unemployment rate is low by historical standards.

What's new and harder to grasp is that, in many places and in many companies, there have been sudden and massive job eliminations. Not selective layoffs over several weeks or months that are only temporary, but complete, permanent shutdowns of entire business units with literally no warning. Hundreds of thousands of people have been dumped in this way. It's the new way of doing business in America. It's being done by individual terminations, voluntary or involuntary early retirements, and large-scale firings. Some of those cut will be able to successfully scramble to new jobs in other business units of the same company, but most will not. It is a form of corporate musical chairs.

This is so very different from past experience that it has shocked the people who are affected by it. As shocked as they are, they must respond differently than they have in the past if they are to survive. Some will have to recognize quickly that they may never again be able to work at what they have been doing for many years. Others will have to accept the possibility of significant cuts in income that will last for several years. Increased competition in almost every sector of the economy means that only the most productive, profitable workers in each area will survive. Jobs that were once thought to require special skills and therefore offer high compensation are moving to other places at lower pay, as the formerly "special" knowledge becomes more common and widespread. And jobs are disappearing completely and regularly, as demand for products and services constantly shifts.

Few people can accept these facts until they have been out of work for many months and been rejected many times. Those who begin to see these new realities must view their recovery and career development differently, and once they're working again, they must be aware that their new jobs could end just as suddenly. Protective measures must be taken.

These measures must include developing other sources of income—and possible future careers—and ways to build a base of financial independence under your family. This independence will require careful planning and hard choices— choices you may not have thought you'd ever have to make. It means, too, that you must become more sensitive to your working environment and particularly to your behavior and to the actions and reactions of those with whom you work.

It means that, if you're married, regardless of whether or not you have children, your spouse must have a regular job. And because of the possibility of fewer and smaller raises, you must be prepared to change jobs more often to keep your income steadily growing.

As much as it may pain you to think about the sacrifices this extra effort will require, it's much more productive to focus on the opportunities it will afford, to acquire new and valuable skills and to exercise options that wouldn't otherwise be open to you. Think of it as a human video cassette recorder. You use this VCR to "time shift," to gradually develop new career opportunities whose value to you and your family lies in the future.

These are some of the important facts of working life in the 1990s. They may not be pleasant to contemplate, but they must be understood and coped with. You will always regret it if you ignore them. But if you recognize them now and use them to your advantage, you'll recover sooner rather than later, and acquire a degree of power to direct your life that you will never relinquish.

The Ax Falls

It will always, *always* come as a surprise. Long after the event, you may look back and see the warning signs you should have recognized before it was too late. For many reasons, however, it won't happen that way. You will be too involved with your work, or will not recognize the warning signs for what they are, or you won't make the connection between a series of warnings. Take my word for it, whether you are given 60 seconds' notice of your termination, or 60 days to choose "early retirement," you will always be surprised. Those who have been terminated more than once know this.

Warning Signs

Noticing these signs won't necessarily prevent your personal Pearl Harbor. With the exception of the first one, no one sign is definite proof of your imminent demise. Several of them should serve to warn you and start you looking for a new job.

1. Average performance evaluations. If that's the best you can do, you're in the wrong job. You may survive, but that's all, and in today's environment, you're not likely to last long. No matter what your superiors tell you

("Somebody has to be average"), this is the single most important red flag that can be waved in your face.

2. Slower-than-average promotions. Find out what the "normal" time for advancement is when you take the job. You'll be given a range: two to three years, for example. If it takes you longer, look for other signs.

3. Salary increases that lag behind those received by your peers. What is the range? Are your increases below it?

4. Lack of challenging assignments. Month after month you are being given the menial, routine assignments that nobody else wants, while your peers are working on tough, high-visibility projects.

5. You're repeatedly "lent out" for other assignments that leave you playing catch-up when you return.

6. You're "offered" transfers that nobody else considers part of an upward career path.

7. Your rate of promotion is at least average, but, relative to your peers, you are falling behind.

8. You have just one major falling out with a superior or a peer who's considered more valuable than you are. You may be a forgiving soul; don't count on others being so charitable.

9. None of the above. It may be that when a choice had to be made, someone else was thought to be more excellent. Sorry 'bout that.

10. The ominous silence. In any large organization, cutbacks do not happen overnight. The numbers to be cut have to be decided on, then those numbers have to be allocated among departments, then individuals

have to be selected. Often, a gag rule is imposed on the managers who'll be involved in the selection process. In the face of this enforced silence, how can you tell if you might be one of "the chosen"?

One way is to ask. If the response is a recitation of the gag rule and nothing else, and you can't get reassurances from any other source, it's a near certainty that you're either on the list or close to being put on it. If you are one of those the company wants to keep, they will find a way to get that message to you, gag rule or no. If all you're told is, "I can't tell you anything," you must realize that, of course, you have just been told all that you need to know.

There are so many ways an imaginative management can get the bad news to you: In the mail. By messenger, in the form of a security guard who hands you a dismissal notice and tells you you have to be packed and out of the building in 20 minutes. From a superior who hasn't the guts to come right out and say what he's doing: "Uh, Tom, you know those expense reductions we've all been hearing about, they're affecting you . . ." "I know, Joe, my expense account's been cut in half." "Uh, no, Tom, it's a bit more than that . . ." Or, even more bizarrely, you are asked to attend a "meeting" in a conference room on another floor. You go into the room only to find out that everyone there is being fired. This is the "Roach Motel" approach to firing: You check in as an employee, you check out as an ex-employee. Terminations, especially on a large scale, are brutal business, and there's no way to pretend that they are anything else.

Individuals can be separated from a job more gracefully and with less pain than is commonly being done today. If it's done right, no one may ever know that the "transfer to another job" was anything but voluntary. Unfortunately, there's no way to sugar coat or hide a large number of involuntary separations.

(I happen to believe strongly that large-scale staffing reductions can be done effectively voluntarily, but that may be of small comfort to you now.)

One strong piece of advice when you are given "the news": *Do not try to change their minds; do not argue.* Accept what is happening to you, even if you do not understand it. It is over; as far as that company is concerned, you are history.

Keep your dignity and your composure. The best attitude is one of icy disdain that stops just short of contemptuous anger. You do not have to do anything to make those who are terminating you feel comfortable. You don't have to agree with anything they are saying, or even respond to it. And don't sign anything, even if you're assured it's just an "acknowledgment" of what you've been offered as outplacement benefits. If you're told your signature is required, put the document in your pocket and say you *may* sign it after you've reviewed it. Say nothing more. Then have your attorney review it. You may be told that if you don't sign the acknowledgment at once, your entry into the outplacement program will be delayed. This tactic is as sleazy as it is misleading. At the moment you aren't in a position to consider anything rationally. A delay of a few days in beginning outplacement counseling isn't going to be fatal to your recovery.

There are many other ways you can react to the event, some of them rational, some of them stupid. You will be shocked, numb, frustrated, angry. No, not just angry; mad. Mad as hell. Cat-kicking mad. You may imagine yourself harming your superiors in every way imaginable.

Fine. Feel angry. Towering rage can be a useful stimulant. Just use it, don't let it use you. Get even. Get even by rising to greater heights than would ever have been possible if you stayed in your old career.

After you've imbued yourself with this determination, after you've charged yourself up to get even by succeeding spectacularly, pause, take a deep breath, and recognize that some of the most trying times of your life are ahead. You may be one of the lucky ones, one of those who'll find a new job in weeks if not days. The odds, though, are against that happening. From most reports, the chances are you're going to be out of work anywhere from two to six months—or longer. But in the end you will prevail; you can count on it.

As the weeks become months you will find that you are doing a lot of waiting: for contacts to get back to you, for résumés to be evaluated, for interviews to be arranged. Waiting is excruciatingly painful, because an important part of your future is now in the hands of others, and you're powerless to change that.

Wait until:

- You've been "on the beach" six months or a year.

- You've been offered 30 percent less than you were making to work for someone half as qualified as you are.

- You have been told, for the seventh time, that you are "overqualified" (i.e., too old—I'm sorry, age discrimination is as pervasive as it is subtle) for a job you know you can do well.

- You have to spend part of a day each week standing on line to sign up for an unemployment check.

- It's necessary to go down to your bank and negotiate face-to-face with a painfully sympathetic loan officer about restructuring the terms of your house mortgage or car loans.

You will wait and wait and wait. You will have to learn to be more humble, patient, and polite than you had to be before.

But your recovery will succeed; this isn't the Great Depression. There are opportunities out there that you might never discover if you didn't have to go out and look for them. When you do succeed, you will realize that you are a better, stronger, more resourceful person coming out of the recovery process than you were going in.

Some people are incredibly resilient. No matter what misfortune confronts them in life, no matter how unexpected or difficult or prolonged it is, they just keep plowing ahead, utterly serene in the belief that ultimately they will prevail.

But not everybody is that optimistic. Some, at some point, will start losing the ability to cope. You will begin to realize that, for instance, when you go out to get your mail one noontime feeling quite upbeat and note for no particular reason that you've been through two six packs of beer so far that morning. Or you may start to believe that things are never going to get any better. That belief will cause you great pain. The pain may become palpable, a deep, hard ache that won't go away. You could start to genuinely doubt everything good you ever felt about yourself. And you then could wind up making the last big mistake of your life, because it is so easy to do, with pills or a gun, or . . .

If you ever think like this for longer than five seconds, *Get help!* Where? *Anywhere someone will listen to you.* Some people draw strength from a religious faith. Others join support groups. Find something you are comfortable with. But get help, *fast.*

The possibility that you might sink to this level of despair is something you ought to consider while you're in a position to think about it rationally. Think about it, in this case, before it's too late. There's no avoiding the fact that until you get back on your feet again and have taken control of your career you're not going to feel great. For that, as *Reader's Digest* has been saying for many years, laughter is the best medicine.

Truly it is. Nothing will help you more than regular doses of laughter. Every once in a while it's helpful to stop, put aside your necessary seriousness, and laugh at your situation. There is lots of "funny" help available; in the comic strips, in local comedy clubs, in the newspapers in such columns as Dave Barry's, and in cartoon books. These are great pressure relievers, and used for that purpose they will help move your recovery along.

Settling Up

There is one important piece of business that has to be negotiated before leaving: the separation package. This is an especially painful time to negotiate, something your ex-employer's counting on. You'll feel mortified and will want nothing more than to get the hell out of there. But you must make the effort, however painful it may be. You may have to negotiate hard for the best package, and if you can't this once dig in your heels and do so, you will always be sorry.

What you're negotiating for is a continuation of salary and all benefits, for as long as possible. Anything less than two weeks' compensation for every year of service is shabby treatment indeed, and even two weeks per year is pretty shabby, given the length of today's job searches. Some people think a week per year is adequate, but they haven't been out job hunting lately.

Here's a tip that can save you a lot of money. You *do not* want to be continued on salary for X weeks. You *do* want the benefits continued for as long as possible, and you *do* want the paychecks sent to you every two weeks for the duration of your severance agreement. But you want your ex-employer to state in writing that that amount is *severance* or *separation pay*. That way you will not have to wait until the date the checks stop coming to begin collecting unemployment compensation; you can start getting those funds after your state's normal waiting period, which can range from two to four weeks.

Remember, if you are offered less than two weeks' pay for every year of service, you are being treated very badly. That may seem like a lot to some people, but unless you're as well networked as Dan Rather it's going to be hard to find a job in a hurry. It will take time, so it's imperative to get the largest possible cushion. What other benefits you will want the company to continue depends on such factors as your age, profession, and whether or not your spouse works. If so, you might for example become covered under his or her health insurance plan, in which case that's one benefit you could afford to negotiate away.

Pay is most important, and if you think what has been offered is not enough, by all means take your case to the next higher level in the organization. The next executive up the line will know about your situation; that person probably initiated or had to sign off on your departure, and you need to meet with them quickly. Your case should be presented with all the poise you can muster and based on your reading of the situation. Review your accomplishments in detail, and if at all possible in terms of their dollar benefit to the company. Make the best case for what you want compared to what's being offered, and await a response. If the answer is, "What you're being given is really the industry norm," or, "You have no idea how tight things are around here now," you may be out of luck. But if the response is something like "Thank you for your candor; we'll get back to you in a couple of days," you may have a chance of getting a better deal. But remember that your immediate boss will not be pleased that you have gone over his or her head. If this person is particularly malicious, he or she could make it more difficult for you to get a new job. That's a risk you have to evaluate.

If you think you're getting a raw deal you may want to consider if it is worthwhile to have a lawyer do the negotiating for you. A few years ago, I would have said no, it isn't worth the ill will it's likely to create. Today my response would be, sure, go for it, if certain conditions are present:

- You are over 40. Companies are more concerned than ever about age discrimination. They aren't intimidated by it—they will fight back if you sue—but they are often concerned enough to take steps to avoid litigation. And those steps may include more generous severance than you'd get if you didn't ask. If you're part of a general layoff, check with others who are in the same boat with you. If their severance package is in any way better, let your lawyer know.

• The stakes are large enough, possibly involving a substantial cash settlement, extended or enhanced benefits, or other large cash-equivalent benefits that are important to you. Hiring an attorney to negotiate for an extra month of severance pay isn't likely to be cost-effective unless that result can be achieved with a telephone call. But the possibility of a consulting contract on top of the severance package, or several months of extended fringe benefits, could justify the use of an attorney.

• The lawyer has experience and a good track record on such matters. An inexperienced lawyer is worse than useless in this area, and will only serve to make you look more foolish.

• You can make some arrangement to pay the lawyer partly or completely, later—when you're up and running again.

If your answers to these questions are positive, there's another step you need to take before looking for a lawyer: arrange a meeting with someone in your nearest state or federal civil rights office or Equal Employment Opportunity Commission to discuss your circumstances, the grievances you think may be justified, and what recourse they think you might have.

If you come away from this meeting more convinced than ever of your righteousness, then you have two choices: Let the government agency decide how best to proceed with your case (a deliberate, time-consuming process), or talk with an advocate.

By advocate, of course, I mean a lawyer specializing in labor law and wrongful discharge. Do not just pick a name from the Yellow Pages. Make inquiries among other lawyers. The lawyers you select to interview should have been recommended to you by at least two people with firsthand knowledge of their capabilities. You do not need a legal scholar or a detached, Olympian perspective on your problems. You want someone who can analyze your situation quickly and tell you honestly if you have a case, and then, if necessary, follow through in a hard-nosed and tenacious manner.

Such advice does not come cheap. Expect to pay at least $150 to $200 an hour. Figure two hours, maximum, for a good initial consultation, and that's assuming you've spelled out the facts and keyed in on the relevant sections of the law as a result of your discussions with the EEOC. You do not want to spend more than this amount of time assessing your situation with a lawyer—tilting at windmills can be a major distraction.

If you decide not to proceed further, you will at least have the peace of mind that comes from knowing you got the best advice available. Then you can move on to more important things. But if your lawyer thinks you have a strong case and that the potential monetary damages could be substantial (especially in relation to your likely legal fees), then by all means go ahead.

Bear in mind, though, that the odds are against you. Most companies are extremely careful in laying the legal foundations for their discharges, and determine at the outset to fight tooth and nail any actions brought against them. And who do you think has the deeper pockets?

Honoring Your Contract

If you're in an industry where employment contracts are common—financial services, communications, for example— you may have a contract that includes important provisions such as those covering separation. Other provisions you may have negotiated might include base salary and any compensation that is deferred or incentive-based, and the means by which your performance will be evaluated.

As you may have recognized, though, nothing is more important than clear termination language. Just what this language should provide for will depend on your particular circumstances. For instance, if you're in a particularly senior position or one that is highly specialized or has notably high turnover, full compensation for at least a year should be provided in the event of termination. For a professional in her or his late fifties or early sixties, an option for retirement should be part of the package.

The important point here is that any provisions are worthless if they can't be enforced. As a broad generality, it is possible to terminate any employment agreement, oral or written, "for cause," and then offer separation terms satisfactory to the employer, regardless of what may have been agreed to. Any contract, therefore, should include broad and explicit limitations on the employer's ability to void the termination provisions of the contract. If for any reason your departure is a particularly nasty one, the company may attempt to get around those limitations regardless; but there's no reason to make it any easier for them.

Using Outplacement Counseling

One of the most valuable components of your separation package can be a provision for outplacement counseling. If this service isn't offered, ask for it. If it's not going to be made available, ask for extra money to buy it yourself. It can change your life, by opening a new world of career possibilities to you. That's not the main purpose in such counseling, of course; recovery is. But good counselors can help you start considering your life beyond the next job.

The way most outplacement counseling services work is this: The counseling firm contracts with a company for a package of services on a per capita basis. The fee can range anywhere from $600 to $3,000 per person. The services provided should include the following: counseling, either individually or in groups (depending on your level), in such areas as psychologically adapting to being unemployed; assessing your strengths and weaknesses, likes and dislikes, and your accomplishments; and developing from this assessment a personal marketing plan, beginning with a résumé.

You should also expect assistance in résumé writing; individual or group sessions in such subjects as networking and practice interviewing; individual counseling before and after job interviews; and advice on negotiating compensation packages.

At a minimum you should expect two full days of small group classroom sessions; a one-on-one critique of your résumé; and a "resident counselor" available during the week in the office space you'll be using.

The best outplacement packages will, in addition, include office space, telephones, and secretarial help for two to six months after you have left your job. The psychological benefit of these office services can't be overestimated. In this important respect, one thing hasn't changed: You must still get up every day, get dressed in business clothes, and go into "the office" to the hardest job in your life—finding a new and more rewarding career. No moping around the house, waiting for the phone to ring is permitted; no "hanging out" is allowed.

There are people in outplacement who only go into the "office" one or two days a week, or take planned vacations of two or three weeks before starting in. They are foolish. Unless you are prepared to make this job your number-one priority, your chances of a speedy recovery on the best possible terms will be diminished. Unless you are prepared to be seriously single-minded about controlling your own future, you will once again find yourself just as much at the mercy of others as you are now. You will have wasted valuable time.

To get the most out of outplacement services, you have to use them intelligently.

- People whose judgment I respect say that it is difficult to spend that many hours productively every week at an outplacement office. I agree. But the people I know who got relocated most quickly put in those kinds of hours.

  Be "at the office" five days a week. You will have to work hard, 35 hours a week regularly, until you have found a job. If you haven't organized your job search so that it requires at least that much time, get help from your counselor in organizing and activating the search; you weren't paying attention when these subjects were discussed in the outplacement class.

- Although you may not have much choice in this matter, try to work with a counselor who's similar to you in age, sex, experience, and educational background, because this will minimize the time you spend establishing communications with this person. Work the counselors hard. They'll be handling other clients, but you should ask for all the help you think you need to get a new job. Don't waste their time with problems that could be better handled by a bartender or a minister; you'll turn them off. They respond best to strivers, not whiners.

- Early on, discuss your wildest career fantasies: anything you've ever wanted to do, but thought you'd sound stupid asking about. Now's the time; you have nothing to lose. Your counselor may be able to give you helpful suggestions that could point you toward a real career change, or advice on developing other interests into money-earning activities. Or, they may point out reasons you'd never think of why you're likely to fail. Either way, the benefit of a second opinion is invaluable.

This is an important point at the beginning of your search. You need help in assessing your options. You should be concerned about your chances of quickly finding work in the area in which you've been looking. Most outplacement counselors are knowledgeable about the techniques of job searches. They aren't aptitude assessment specialists and they may not know much about your industry, so they may not be able to answer your questions. They should be able to steer you to people who can, either in their own organizations or elsewhere. If a move to a different part of the country interests you, they should be able to put you in touch with associates in that area who can advise you on the local situation. And if they can't do that, they should at least be able to save you time in seeking out people with the answers you need. It's important that these issues be settled to your satisfaction before the serious work of your search starts. Otherwise they'll be an unneeded distraction.

• Coaching in interviewing techniques is particularly important. You need more than a list of likely questions and preferred answers. You can certainly benefit from one-on-one coaching in deliberately stressful simulated interviews. These should be videotaped and played back to you if at all possible. If you survive the shock, you'll learn a great deal that you can use when you go knocking on doors. Pay close attention to your personal mannerisms and your language skills. If verbal communication hasn't been your forte, you will have to polish your skills before you go too much farther. The personal skills needed in everyday job situations are not the ones you'll need when you have to go out alone and sell yourself to strangers; you will be initiating and acting—not reacting.

• Don't let the recovery process get you down. "Cold calling" and the high level of rejection that goes with it can be depressing. So although it's important to put in those 35-hour weeks, when you really get discouraged, get out of the office. Do something different—work out or get caught up on your reading until you feel refreshed. Then get back to work.

Two cautionary notes about using outplacement counselors. Remember that they were hired by the people who fired you. Accordingly, when you do accept a job offer, do not share with anyone in any way connected with your old company the terms and conditions you've agreed to. This is information no one who's not a direct party to the transaction needs to have, and if it gets back to your ex-employers, the information could be used to defend any lawsuits you might bring in the future. The chances of that happening are not great, but there is no reason whatsoever to disclose the information. Outplacement firms like to document their "100 percent success" rates in placing clients, but the most you will want to say is you've taken a new job. Period. Good-bye. Thank you.

The same applies to people who are in outplacement with you, people you haven't previously met but who say they are from your company. There is always the possibility of a "ringer" or a "plant," particularly if the number of outplacees is large. It is possible, though farfetched, that someone may be placed in your group with instructions to try to finger potential litigators. If litigation is on your mind, keep it to yourself. The same applies to any information about job offers you've received or are considering. You have nothing to gain and potentially a lot to lose by sharing this information with those who aren't close confidants of long standing.

Above all, when you accept a job offer and no longer need counseling or the outplacement office, just leave, without saying anything to anyone. Just stop showing up. This is not how you'll want to depart. You'll want to shout the good news to anyone within earshot. But restrain yourself. Confine the good news to those you've known and trusted for years.

CHAPTER TWO

Taking Stock After the Shock

Now you are out the door, on the street. You turn and look back at the place where you've spent 5, 10 or more years of your working life. You are alone, embarrassed, frustrated. You have a long hard job ahead of you.

You are going to feel numb. Your head is rolling across the floor after the ax has fallen, and you recognize that fact, but the reality of it is so painful to contemplate that you cannot accept it. That is *just* how you will feel. Few experiences in life are more devastating. A death in the family, incarceration—only those experiences are more painful than being terminated.

There is a difference, however: There *is* life after this death. Recognizing that mundane truth will come as an exhilarating revelation in the midst of your despair. During your recovery, you will have great days and black-hole days as you start to climb back up. If you have a family, its ties will be stretched. If you have a religious faith, its strength will be tested.

Like being born and dying, this is something you must do yourself. At your old company, you never existed. When your name comes up at all, you are referred to in the hushed past tense reserved for those who passed on long ago, of causes too unpleasant to mention. You cannot imagine how invisible you will quickly become, how soon your former friends at the office will forget they ever knew you. That is one of the most depressing aspects of being outplaced. The great part is that you will also learn who your true friends are, and with them, you will be able to share your new and better life.

If you are to ascend once again to the living world, you must now do something that you may never have done before: You have to be totally honest with yourself, about yourself.

The world is filled with men and women who made a career of rolling on from one difficult job environment to another, never learning, never changing, never adapting, because they could never face the reality of their own selves. They have gone on through life as if they were the captain of the next *Titanic*, saying, "This time, we'll keep a sharper lookout."

Mistakes? Who, Me?

You have to learn from your mistakes, and the first step is admitting that you made mistakes. It's highly likely that they contributed to your downfall. Once you can accept that, you will have taken a big step on the road to recovery, for if there is one thing you want to do, it's minimize the number of mistakes you make more than once. Now is the time to consider what mistakes you made. You had to make a few, or you wouldn't have been terminated. How do you think firings happen? The decision is made that X number of people have to be cut. Then a list of potential candidates is made. How did your name get on the list? Right—you helped put it there.

Your biggest mistake, the most likely reason for your firing, probably had to do with your own personality. That may be hard to accept, but it is the truth or mostly the truth. The most important thing you do every day is not say your prayers or hug your wife or pat the dog, but curry favor with the right people. That is the essence of an effective business personality. What's most important? Talent? Initiative? Organizational ability? They count for a great deal, but without a personality to go with them, they are not enough. Besides, having an agreeable personality is not necessarily the same thing as being a busser of butts.

Now, let's not make too big a deal out of this. There's an old Pennsylvania Dutch saying, "Everyone is crazy but thee and me, and sometimes I wonder about thee." It's easy to believe that you are the one normal person in a warped world; that everyone has a weird personality except you. It's when you start acting on that belief that you open yourself to potential trouble. You don't have to have the personality of an ogre to get in trouble today; unintended abrasiveness will do it for you.

That is exactly what happened to a former colleague of mine a few years ago. He had what you'd call a "prickly" personality; he did not suffer fools gladly. This didn't bother many of the people he worked with because despite his attitude he was an exceptionally knowledgeable and useful professional. But a corporate reorganization sent him to another part of the company where the local corporate culture was easygoing, polite, and unfailingly courteous. They saw no reason to put up with his attitude and didn't think any level of knowledge justified it. They worked with him to the extent they had to, but he never got the message. As a result, his performance slipped. He never became an integral part of his new team, and when the requirement for cutbacks arose, he was one of the first to go. And he was and is a very nice guy!

The chances are that you have acquired some noticeably irritating personality traits over the years. The following are extreme forms of defects, but they'll help you to see your own subtler and correctable flaws: You're too loud, or you never contribute anything; you're the office comedian, or you never laugh at anyone else's jokes; you try to get brownie points by being the first one in and the last to leave, or you are a clock-watcher, out the door at the stroke of 5:00 P.M.

The worst habits by far are those of talking too much and not listening enough. The Loudmouth, the pushing, garrulous, opinionated character who is always interjecting him- or herself into your conversation, is an overloaded truck speeding downhill with no brakes.

So is the Nonlistener. While not as overtly offensive as the Loudmouth, he is as irritating in his own special way. You know him: he never lets you finish anything. You start to ask him a question, he finishes asking it for you and answers it without pausing for breath, so smart is he. Or, you will be talking to him about a special problem and his response will be a discourse on something completely unrelated. The Nonlistener will get back to your problem, eventually, but not until he's cleared his own mind.

These are two facets of what's obviously a self-centered person, but people in dead-end jobs tend to get that way, having long ago given up any hope of anyone else recognizing their importance. The point is, everyone displays *some* of these characteristics from time to time. The more frustrated in your job you feel, the more likely they are to surface in your everyday behavior. That's when your situation starts to become precarious. You don't even have to feel frustrated. You just have to have a personality trait that's guaranteed to annoy and offend others.

At the very least, having an agreeable personality means two *nots*: not being offensive and not being aloof. You do not have to be the most ingratiating person on earth, and you do not have to be as rapt a listener as your Confessor down at St. Ignatz. What you do have to avoid is being offensive.

Offensive is rarely the same thing as insulting, and all of us offend in different ways. Here are some of the ways—subtle and not-so-subtle—I've learned about. Built up over time, these offenses can help tilt the balance against you.

- Debating everything your boss tells you. You may think she wants full and open discussion, or that she wants to see that her subordinates can think for themselves. It's as likely, though, that she wants her own conclusions reinforced. You have to find out what these are, cautiously, and then be sure to give her what she wants. The best way to do this is by carefully observing how she's responded to by others who have worked for her for some time. When it's clear your boss genuinely wants your best professional opinion, by all means offer it— but as two or three *possibilities,* not a set-in-concrete view you can't back away from without sounding uncertain or ignorant.

- Making your boss look bad in public. She's just made a big mistake in a sales presentation, and it could cost your team the sale. Do you correct her? Only if you are utterly convinced that the mistake, uncorrected, will actually cost you the sale, and *then* only if you can do so without offending her. Passing a note or making a face may do it. Otherwise, *don't do it.* The risks to you are too great.

- Joking about The Company. It's common today to joke about one's employer: "Did you hear about the Saudi prince whose kid wanted a Mickey Mouse outfit for his birthday, so he bought him this company?" That may be common, but to a lot of old-timers, including the Key Player (see Chapter 11) it is the worst of bad manners.

- Not cooperating. There is a person in your department who has the same rank as you. Sometimes you work together, sometimes independently. But you just do not get along with this person. You are diametric opposites, so you assume the prudent course of action is to avoid or ignore him. WRONG! Wrong because (a) you may be the only one who has a problem with him, and (b) you're not paid to pick and choose your coworkers. If you're on the same team, go out of your way to treat him as a valued member of the team. It may turn out that he can't work with anyone, in which case he'll be gone before you are.

The ways of giving offense are endless, and there is only one sure rule to follow when you're in doubt as to whether what you want to say will give offense. The cardinal rule is: *Keep your mouth shut. Zip it. Say nothing.*

This is not advice that's so obvious it's dumb even to offer it. People seem to take offense more quickly than they ever did, but you may not be rebuked immediately if you say something that offends someone. If you're in doubt a lot, you may find yourself saying little. That's fine. Just be sure you know the difference between silence and aloofness. You certainly want to go out with the salespeople after work on Friday night for a few beers. You can be good company just by sitting there and laughing at the jokes and asking polite questions that will keep the talkers talking. By all means, go to company parties and other gatherings such as conventions, for two reasons: it shows *you* feel you're part of the Company family, and you want *everyone else* to see it, too. It's not that hard; it doesn't take much extra effort. The second rule is, never say no. No matter how demeaning or dumb you consider a request that's been made by your superior, go along with it. Always.

Having a personality means almost never having to say you're sorry. It means having humility and sensitivity. You have gotten into difficulty at least in part because you didn't get along well enough. No excuses—"Those guys were a bunch of crude SOB's"—are accepted. You can do better. You have to do better.

It can't be emphasized enough, though, that the day of the individual who made it on personality *alone* has passed. Unless personality is a central element of your professional competence, as in sales, reaching constantly higher levels of professional excellence should be your first priority. Just remember

that there are many more well-qualified people available than
there ever have been, and when it comes to choosing, personality may well be the deciding factor.

There are other things you can do to improve yourself that
don't fall strictly into the category of personality. Attitude is
something that can always be improved. You can begin to improve by becoming a better listener. Your manager may not
always like to speak directly about her wishes. You're enough of
a pro, she may feel, that an indirect hint should be more than
enough. So like a radio telescope looking for emanations from
distant life forms, you have to keep tuning back and forth across
her wavelength until you've received her message. Then act on it.

Is the message that you need some additional training? Sign
up for it, pronto. Are you being asked to do something differently or to spend more time on one part of your job? Think
through what this means, then make the changes, then make
sure the changes remain in effect, whether or not you like
them and agree with them. If you have an honest difference
of opinion, of course you should bring it up. But always do
so in a nonconfrontational, nonthreatening manner. Then accept the verdict that is handed down. Your primary task is to
keep your superiors happy even if you aren't always in
agreement. And who knows, you may even learn something
from them. Your responsiveness to their needs and wishes is
what's most important to them, and to you. The way you
respond is as important. Do you rarely respond until you've
been hit up alongside your head with a two-by-four, or are
you always ready to listen willingly? It matters for nothing that
you are 100 percent responsive if getting you to respond is
always a royal pain for someone else.

What You Can't Control. And What You Can

Although you can do things to improve your personality and
your attitude, there are many things that affect your future
that you're powerless to control. There's no sense losing sleep

over them. If consumer tastes shift away from the product your company makes, or if your company gets bought out and the new owners decide to shift production from Kalamazoo to Karachi, there isn't a great deal you can do about it.

What you can do is constantly review the shape your company and industry are in. Is your company thriving, or is it stagnating and vulnerable to liquidation or takeover by an acquisitor who will come in with a meat-ax? Are you working in the 1990s equivalent of the buggy-whip industry? If so, your natural tendency may be to try to hang on to the end, to be the last one out the door. But that will be reacting to the actions of others, not initiating action on your own, and when you do finally see the light, it may be too late.

Keeping track of your company and the industry it's in is worth the effort. If it's a decent sized publicly-held company your job is easier, because information about such matters as finances and sales is made public regularly. So even if you can't affect the quality of your company's management or its economic well-being, you can at least get a fair picture of where it's going.

The place to look for this information is in your local library. If you're at all concerned, begin by reviewing any articles that have been published about the company in the last year in the *Wall Street Journal, Barron's, The New York Times* or your local newspaper, or *Forbes, Fortune,* or *Business Week* magazines. Does a consistent picture emerge? If there are as many negatives as positives, you should be concerned. Are you just not certain? If your company's stock is publicly traded, call around to major brokerage firms to see if their analysts have published any reports on the company's outlook. If its debt has been rated by Moody's or Standard and Poor's, look up their reports on the rationales for the initial ratings, and look for any updated analyses.

After you've considered these "big picture" matters, those that are beyond your control, shift your focus to matters you can control: your skills and your job situation.

Keeping Your Skills

Because the world is changing so fast today, it's deceptively easy to lose your professional skills. It is harder than ever to keep up, but if you don't make the effort, you'll fall back in the pack fast. Just keeping up with computers can be terrifying, but there are so many other ways you can fall behind that you may not realize your skills have become obsolete until it's too late.

Consider the case of a once top-notch financier. A superb people person, he was one of the most effective salesmen I'd ever met. But this didn't help him when new and complicated financing techniques evolved in his specialty, and proved to be greatly beneficial to his clients. He could not or would not master them. He disdained them, always seeking the older, simpler methods. He referred to the new techniques as "bells and whistles" financings. He used that term once too often. He is now selling BMWs.

This is how many people wind up in career dead ends. The requirements of their jobs change—that happens all the time. They don't like or can't master the new requirements of the job. That may be normal, but if you are not systematically acquiring new skills that will help you do your job better, control will slip away from you. You should then consider a different career that interests you enough that you will enjoy keeping up. If you don't relish new challenges and approach conquering them with real zest, you will lose out to others who do bring enthusiasm to work every day.

Unfortunately, many people have no idea of how to acquire the skills needed to keep their jobs or move up the career ladder. Three standard ways to acquire new skills are: on-the-job training, through courses offered by your company, and by taking relevant college courses after work.

On-the-job training enables you to acquire skills that are immediately useful. Just ask the people who know what you want to know to show you. They'll be flattered by your interest, and the points they emphasize will tip you off to what's particularly important about the new skill. Formal courses may be required for advancement, or you may want to volunteer to take them to demonstrate your interest to management; that's fine, but what you learn may be wasted if it can't be put to work right away to raise your performance to a higher level. After-hours courses or a specialized degree may be necessary simply because the degree or certification is a "union card" required for admission to the next higher career level.

Who Do You Work For?

As if keeping current wasn't enough of a challenge, there's something else you need to be aware of as the structure of business changes: of how multiple reporting relationships affect you.

As layers of management disappear, you may find yourself with reporting relationships that are at best confused. You may find that you have to report to more than one superior: your nominal superior, and her boss. The latter may often come to you directly, maybe even work with you directly on assignments. There may be good reasons for this management style, but it is always awkward. You have to do whatever either boss tells you, and you must always keep your immediate superior informed of what her manager has told you to do. That way, when conflicts arise over the use of your time, she will have to decide for you which job gets done first.

A really good manager practices "management by walking around," according to Tom Peters. She will try to keep in contact with many of those who work for her, whether or not there's a direct reporting relationship. You have a dilemma, however, when your ultimate superior tells you to do a job in a way that you think your immediate boss might not approve of.

In this situation you are on your own. It would be easy to advise you to try to satisfy both of them, but that's not always possible. If you have to choose, do it the way your immediate superior would want it done; she is the one who writes your annual performance reviews. It is with her, too, that you should candidly discuss the problem. No manager, however junior, likes to be put in a position of being second-guessed by her boss. She may not respond to you immediately, but you can bet she will try to get things changed; her career advancement may depend on it.

It's important to assess your skills, your personality, and the way you have handled relationships as you begin your recovery, because these are all critical to sustaining your recovery. You should take into account the insights you have gained about yourself through this process of self-analysis; they should be foremost in your mind as you consider the kinds of job situations you can be comfortable in and succeed in.

The Care and Feeding of Difficult Personalities

The possibility of encountering difficult personalities in the future is something that may be of far less concern to you now than the possibility of encountering any personality bearing a paycheck. However, for just that reason you may ignore the importance of personality as you begin your job search, and this could lead to your being behind the eight ball once again.

One consequence of unremitting competitive pressure in the business world is the rise to prominence of increasing numbers of workers who are exceptional producers but who have one or more severe personality defects. In the past such defects would have prevented these people from rising to any position of responsibility. But competition has forced senior managers to promote producing professionals they previously wouldn't have touched with rubber gloves. This single-minded focus on production and the bottom line is great if you're a stockholder, but it can seriously interfere with your career plans if you have to work with or for these people.

We are not talking about minor eccentrics such as the one who insists on having desk papers arranged just so, or the person who refuses to see you if you are more than two minutes late for an appointment. We're talking about serious anger, erratic behavior, capricious actions, and explosive tempers that can make a working relationship a new challenge every day.

It's obvious, however, that you are the soul of civility—patient, unfailingly courteous, calm, consistent, and a friend to everyone. Nonetheless, you may want to stop polishing your halo for a moment while you consider what you're up against.

Imagine the embodiment of your worst personality nightmares. It could take this form: He's first and foremost a world-class pro. Whether he works in a metropolitan mecca or in Podunk, he is widely respected for the quality of his work. He's an innovator, a technician on the leading edge with new developments, who has the ability to turn those developments into solid profits. His peers respect him.

You work for him. This is what you see: He comes in at 10:00 A.M. (but always works till 7:00 or 8:00 P.M.); he smokes like the chimney on a steel mill—three packs a day of unfiltered Camels are his norm. You know he's a manic-depressive; he crashes from exhilaration to melancholia faster than you can freshen his drink after work. He works killing hours every week. Twenty of those hours he tries to put in at home on the weekends, but with three mischievous kids he has to lock himself in a book-lined closet to get anything done. He is exquisitely polite to you in most face-to-face encounters, but communicates little of what he expects from you. Your annual performance reviews are average or above average, even though by every measure you can think of, you've gotten better and better. Several times a year you are on the receiving end of foaming-at-the-mouth temper tantrums. He alternately delegates everything to you and acts as a control freak—you never know which to expect. In meetings when your peers and supervisors are present he will sometimes react to you as though you have just insulted him, and other times as if you were the savior of the company.

No functioning human being, of course, could embody as many dysfunctional traits as this caricature. But since recognizable variants will be crossing your path regularly, your most positive response lies in learning to work around their handicaps.

The personality warts on this stereotype have been exaggerated so that you will recognize them when you see them, and be able to respond and adapt. There's no suggestion that most of the people you encounter for the rest of your working life are going to be so difficult. But it is likely that you'll encounter people with serious problems who respond to the pressures of daily business life without grace, tact, humor, or anything else warm and fuzzy.

When you have to work for one of these people, your objective should not change: his complete satisfaction; high praise from him. It will be an extra burden to work around your nasty superior's bad points, and to not let him upset you to the point where you lose control and lash back.

As unpleasant as these people can be to work with, their presence in a corner office by no means dooms you to a working life of misery. It's not necessary for you to respond to every second temper tantrum by shooting out résumés or by locking your office door and beating your head against the wall. Only if the corporate culture seems to cultivate and lionize these types and holds them up as models do you need to think about moving on.

I'm sure you will recognize past or present associates in this example. Your first objective is to do your utmost to work closely with them and, when that isn't possible, work around them. If their behavior is consistently abusive and offensive, you shouldn't have to put up with it. How you deal with it then is important to you and could affect your future at the company.

Personal insecurity plagues many new managers today. They lack the equanimity that longtime tenure brings to most professionals. Unless you're a glutton for punishment, do not do anything that adds to their insecurity. This means:

Avoid anything that they might interpret as confrontational. This means not only that you avoid pushing arguments past the first sign of resistance on their part; it means couching virtually all your conversation in the most supportive possible terms, and restating those terms often. Not, "This is what I think," but "You've stated that our objective is . . . here are a few thoughts that might help us reach that objective." Such small differences can make a big difference in how you are perceived: as understanding and supportive or as a potential obstacle.

When asked for your opinion, express it as two or more options, never as the only possible answer: "Here are some of the possibilities: there's A; briefly, its advantages and disadvantages are . . ." Keep your response as brief as possible without making it sound simplistic.

Keep your disagreements to yourself. If a colleague asks you, "Don't you think our new boss is a bit off the wall?" don't respond. If pressed, say simply, "Every boss has her own way of doing things; I'm sure we'll pick up on hers soon." You may, of course, think she is totally unsupportable, but you have nothing to gain now and almost everything to lose by expressing such a view.

Once you are certain that your persistent efforts to be Ms. or Mr. Congeniality in an exceptionally difficult situation have been noticed by others but haven't produced a positive change in behavior, what's next? Three steps: First, when you get to the point where unacceptable (to you) behavior is becoming more frequent and getting more unpleasant, start a log of incidents. Every time you are dumped on, take detailed notes of the event, including circumstances leading up to the unacceptable behavior, other people (if any) who were present, and exact quotations of language you consider offensive.

Dates, times, and locations should also be included in your records.

As you build up this record, it's still important not to share your concerns with anyone else, even if they witnessed your being dumped on, even if they have been a witness more than once.

The second step is to pick an appropriate time to confront your tormentor head on. The appropriate time will be near the end of an especially nasty harangue, when you sense, based on your previous experience, that it is winding down. You are now going to respond, but *not* in kind. You are going to say what needs to be said, what you have every right to say; and what, if said in the right way *may* (the odds are perhaps 50-50; no better) defuse the situation and prevent future incidents.

You want to sound firm but polite; angry just beneath the surface, but completely in control of your emotions. You want to interrupt the tirade while it is still going on, but after its fury is spent. Some say when you pick the time to respond, do it at the beginning of the storm before it builds up. I think it's more effective if you give the offender one last time to listen to himself, then nail him as he's running out of breath.

Now it is your turn: "Stop, stop! I've supported you in every way I could since we started working together. My performance has exceeded your requirements in every respect, and I've worked my tail off to help this team achieve its objectives. But even if I hadn't, there would be no way to justify your repeated confrontational responses, your uncontrolled temper tantrums, and your totally unprofessional and inhumane methods of communication. You have been disrespectful in the extreme and I've put up with it for as long as I intend to. I'm leaving the office right now. I hope you understand and appreciate my determination not to be treated so contemptuously and unprofessionally ever again. And if you want to resume on a more civilized plane, I'll be in my office."

Your voice level throughout is one clear notch above conversational, but not close to yelling; your tone, emphatic and fast paced but not nearly so rushed as to sound panicky. Your hands remain in your lap; eye contact is maintained until you turn to leave.

Your declaration of self-respect will evoke one of three responses. The response may be nothing; nada; silencio. Such personality types have a large element of the bully in them, so your strong response may be completely unexpected, and any sort of response, even a restrained apology, may be long in coming. There is a chance that you'll receive in due time something approaching a formal, even grateful apology. You'll be called in, the office door will be shut, and into your wondering ears will come words like, "Look, I want to apologize for my recent behavior toward you. I realize now that your response the other day was fully justified and a long time in coming. I was aware of my behavior, but obviously not aware of how painful it must have been. I guess I rationalized it as being appropriate in the circumstances, given the heavy pressure we've been under recently. I'll try hard to avoid any repeat performances, but in the future please let me know immediately if something bothers you."

Thank you, sir, you say to yourself, that took more than a little courage. My respect for you just went up two notches. It'll stay up there if you do avoid backsliding. Now—I'm outta here!

It's also possible that you will be fired so quickly that the normal termination described in Chapter One will by comparison seem like a slow-motion minuet. The likelihood of that possibility is something you must assess before responding directly to terminally gross and crude behavior. Some enterprises do have a culture that, at the very least, tolerates such behavior in certain high-level or high-producing individuals.

Toleration may be taken as acceptance, so the practice may be widespread if not pervasive. When your reading of the situation tells you that this is the case, you probably don't have or shouldn't exercise the option of going on to Step Three in this process, which is a meeting with the most senior personnel or human resources officer with whom you're acquainted, even casually. In those cases where out-of-bounds behavior seems to always be in bounds, my experience has been that there's nothing you can do to change it. If you can't live with the situation and work around it, start planning to get out.

Going to Personnel

Assuming, however, that you are neither apologized to nor fired, your next move should be into the personnel offices, not later than two to three days after your confrontation. Why personnel, why not your antagonist's boss? Why not wait longer for a response? And what do you then say to the personnel person?

For several good reasons it's best at this juncture to go to a senior staff person rather than up the chain of command. Right now, a primary objective should be to make sure your concerns are heard, but handled discreetly. That may not be possible if you go to your boss' boss. And, it's critically important that you be able to separate what was said from the manner in which it was said. It is the latter that implicitly or explicitly is violating the company's personnel policies. A human resources professional will see that distinction and recognize its importance. A line officer may not or may not care.

You should still be very much interested in avoiding confrontation. That may seem to contradict the advice I've just given you, which is to bring about a confrontation, but it isn't. You had no choice but to confront unacceptable actions; you should choose now to limit the confrontation, if possible, by going first to the personnel specialist. Finally, protecting your interests is important at this juncture. When you finish your presentation to the personnel person, it's highly unlikely that your concerns will be taken lightly, even though it would be easy for a senior manager to misread them as whining or as just part of a personality clash that he shouldn't have been drawn into.

Why not wait before going into personnel? Why not give things a chance to simmer down a little? Won't taking this next step so soon be seen as a slap in the face, a failure on your part to see if the offensive behavior ends? That's a chance you will have to take. The chance you don't want to take is on the possibility of a preemptive strike by your boss. You have to consider the likelihood of his reacting to your response by initiating disciplinary action or a termination procedure against you, on whatever grounds he can concoct in a hurry. He may move faster than you do, but your quick action will ensure that you get a fair hearing. Besides, unless you get a complete apology almost immediately, it's important to go on record with personnel to complete the process.

Your presentation to personnel should be concise and specific. Describe the objectionable behavior objectively and in detail, then explain why you think it's unacceptable. This may be evident from your descriptions, but your main points should be emphasized. From your log, repeat word-for-word the most offensive examples, together with all the details. Do not provide the names of witnesses unless you are asked for them.

Certainly note that you've addressed the problem with the offender, but that you now feel a great need to share your concerns with someone else. Be clear in your desire to have things corrected—to affect remedial action—but also make explicit your deep concern at how far the situation has deteriorated. This can be done by asking for advice on other options such as transfers, while you are soliciting insights as to how you can help improve your current situation.

Say exactly what you feel. It should be clear from what you have said that your concerns are deeply felt; that it is your team spirit and your desire to patch things up that have kept you from filing a formal complaint.

You may get some good feedback during the meeting, advice on remedial actions you can take. Try them if you think they will work. If you have a solid record within the company, chances are good that your concerns will be taken seriously. Through more than one channel the offender will be spoken to, and you may not need to say another word on the subject. You are betting that your version of events will be largely accepted and corrective action quietly initiated as a matter of corporate policy.

What if there's no improvement? After a decent interval, return to personnel. Mention the lack of change and inquire again, this time more persistently, about available transfers. Then, if the situation doesn't improve dramatically, renew your job search.

Having done all this, the question has to be asked, is there any way this whole exercise could have been avoided? Is there anything I could have done earlier on that would have made this near-final confrontation unnecessary? Well, there is something you could have tried. After the first few offenses, after you've discerned a pattern that bothers you, you could have tried then to bring it to a head by using a more low-key version of the speech you gave when you finally fought back. At this point, you still don't want to be confrontational, but you are trying to send a serious message. So your tone must be light without being frivolous, plainspoken but not caustic.

"Hey, hey, hey—was all that really necessary? You hurt me, boss. Come on, we don't need that." That's all. If your message has been received, the response should be soon in coming: "Hey, I hear you; sorry 'bout that." The congenital bully's game is to keep punching: two shoves, one step back; so any improvement may be short-lived. But any is better than none, and not allowing a deteriorating situation to get out of hand may be the best course of all. The problem is, not everyone feels artful enough in discourse to bring this off without sounding confrontational. Consequently, they hesitate to try.

Moving On

We've just seen examples of serious situations in which you may have found yourself in the past. If at all possible, they should be avoided in the future. At this very beginning stage of your recovery, such matters may be far in the back of your mind. A job, any good job, is most important. Once you have the job, then you can concern yourself with personality issues. You think.

The problem, of course, is that by then it may be too late, and may delay, if not derail, the completion of your recovery on your terms. This is why as you begin the job-search part of your recovery, you should remember the importance of learning as much as possible about the people with whom you will be working. This isn't always easy to do, but a little ingenious inquiring can usually produce the information you need. People like to talk about other people, the bad as well as the good. When you find out what "the bad" is in any given situation, you can determine whether "the good" more than compensates for what you'll have to put up with.

All the issues discussed in this chapter are important to laying the foundation for your recovery. Environmental awareness is critically important to a successful recovery, particularly when that environment is an intensely competitive, highly pressurized business office. There is no way you can survive today if you don't develop an acute sensitivity to what is going on around you all the time. This sensitivity and all that it encompasses is as important as a high level of professional competence.

CHAPTER THREE

Starting Back

The first thing you have to do after being separated is put into place a **Transition Budget**. This is a plan of expenditures based on what you know your income will be in the period you are unemployed. What period? This may come as a jolt, but you'd better plan on a year. Your highest hope is that you will not need that long. You should try hard to get back to work within 60 days, but with all the competition in the job market, the budget you make should carry you through a much longer period.

Your severance package should include full or partial pay and benefits for anywhere from two weeks to six months. After your severance pay ends you will fall off a financial cliff. Your only financial safety net will be your savings and state unemployment benefits, and those benefits will not carry you very far if you haven't figured out how to stretch your other dollars.

The trick is not to stretch them so far that they break. Here are some ideas that will make your funds go farther:

- Go back over every cash outlay and every check you've sent out in the last three months and categorize each expenditure: housing, transportation, utilites, dues, charity, and such. Then reduce the categories to two: Essen-

tial and Deferrable. You must decide which is which in
your situation.

It is quite possible that from all the categories you will
be able to identify hundreds if not thousands of dollars
of potential savings. These savings are worth taking now.
From country-club memberships to magazine subscrip-
tions, they add up. Be brutal in canceling all that you
can, recognizing that the cuts and cancelations are only
temporary. You're going to eat out less, buy fewer
clothes, take fewer trips. Until you're back and recovered
you must spend less.

• Don't go out and buy a less-expensive house—at least not
now. Doing so may save you money in the long run, but
in the short run—one year—it's unlikely that it will save
enough to offset the transaction costs—the costs you'll
incur in selling your house and buying a new one. Selling
the house is something you may have to begin to think
about after you've been out of work a year—maybe.

• Don't sell your car. Even if it's almost new and has a lot
of undepreciated value in it, sell it only if it's a luxury
car and you can net some big savings: Sell it for $30,000,
cash, move down to something in the $17,000 range, and
bank the difference. Do that if you can; otherwise, hold
on to your old, paid-for clunker; you'll need it.

• If your cushion of savings is thin, think about taking a
part-time job when your state unemployment benefits
run out, usually 6 to 12 months. Until then your job
search is your full-time job. If you're married and your
spouse is not working, adding that second job should be
done immediately (if, that is, you'll be ahead financially
after taking into account new expenses such as day care).

• From now until the recovery is complete, spend nothing
casually. You have no "discretionary" income. Every dollar that isn't needed for an "essential" expenditure is

hoarded. If for no other reason than the light it may shed on your expenditure patterns, you may want to start a ledger in which every outlay is recorded.

• Cut yourself a little slack. Don't wipe out all your pleasures. Decide which of them you enjoy the most, and set aside funds for once-a-month enjoyment of them. This will give you a useful psychological lift, something to look forward to when you'll need it most.

The Transitional Budget has to go into effect immediately. Then you can start planning for the future. Start by locking yourself up in your home for a long weekend to review everything about the situation you're now in. Disconnect the phone. If the children are old enough for their input to be considered, include them; otherwise, it should be just you and your spouse. No subject should be off limits: relocation, career change, lifestyle change. Just keep the discussions moving on two tracks: What we'd like to do, and what we have to do to start a new paycheck coming in within 60 days.

Relocation?

If you've developed a serious interest in relocating, a move can be one of the options you consider. A serious interest means:

• You've visited an area many times and thoroughly enjoyed it each time.

• You've recently checked out, in depth, the local job and housing markets, compared them favorably in almost every way to where you live now, and concluded you would miss nothing you'd be leaving behind.

• Most important, you've made and maintained some professional contacts, contacts you can now use to help get a new job.

If you've done all this, you may still have to face one large obstacle. Many employers will say to someone who's thinking about immigrating: "It's great that you're interested. Call us when you're settled here." When you've relocated, not before.

If you decide you do want to move, you can conduct a thorough long-distance job search in the destination of your choice, but don't get your heart set on being successful. A job is your number-one priority. Not the ideal job—not now, at any rate.

But you may have a particularly strong professional interest in relocating. You may not want to consider a career change. And the only way to do that may be by moving to another part of the country. Maybe you're so career centered that where you live doesn't matter, as long as the job situation is right for you. Or possibly you don't feel you have the luxury of choice; you've simply concluded you have to move.

Since it is easy to make a move you'll hate yourself for, you should research the possibilities if time and money aren't critical concerns; in other words, if you're still employed. Then we'll see how to condense the process while still improving your chances of making a good choice, even though you're unemployed.

First, buy a seven-day-a-week mail subscription to the largest paper in the area to which you're considering relocating. Over time this will provide you with much of the information you need to begin to make a decision: the availability of your kind of jobs; local property prices and taxes; schools; politics; cultural and recreational activities; and community services.

Visiting and Assessing a Community

Then, visit the area when it's least attractive. For Florida, this means July and August; for Minnesota, January or February. Can you tolerate the heat or the snow? Do you think your family will be able to?

On this trip and on one other, you have to get more information: firsthand knowledge of the job, school, and housing situations. You'll need to spend several days tracking down job leads you've gleaned from the classified ads, and talking to employment agencies and executive recruiters. At the end of this trip you should have come to some conclusions as to whether or not you'll be better off—or at least as well off professionally and financially.

If by this time you aren't convinced that there are real opportunities available, start thinking about another area. And if you are really attracted to your first choice, but more than a little put off by the job prospects, start thinking about the trade-offs that would be involved in a move.

Checking out the job markets is something you can do by yourself on the first trip. On the next trip you have to bring the family, because you will be looking at schools and homes. If you have school-age children, this will answer the other important question: Would I want to live in this area in the kind of home I could afford if the schools are acceptable? Start out on your own, again with the local paper's classified ads. Look for "open houses" and new developments. Then, if you can, spend a half day with a real estate agent looking at homes within your price range. Ask all the important questions about schools, taxes, churches, transportation, environmental issues, and recreation.

You can't be sure where in the area you'll wind up working. So while you're driving around, pay attention to the road network. Can you get around in decent time in all areas? Where are the spots of major congestion and how long do they seem to last? What's being done to alleviate them?

If you're out of work and time and money are tight, one person can do these surveys in about three days, not including travel. If you can't afford the newspaper subscription or don't want to wait for it to start, when you arrive in the area spend a morning at the library reading as many back issues as possible. Having brought many copies of your résumé, distribute them personally to employers, employment agencies, and headhunters the afternoon of Day One. Tell them you'll call back the day after tomorrow. This is an unorthodox approach, but an appropriate one in the circumstances.

Spend the evening of Day One just driving around. All of Day Two should be spent assessing housing; you should have a decent feel for affordability and acceptability by the evening. This may not be possible with respect to the job market. It's possible, even likely, that you'll get zero feedback from your cold calls. Therefore, even if time is critical, it pays to send out résumés and make appointments before you head out.

Please don't get the idea that, even if you're working, it's always possible to choose an area to relocate to on the basis of two long visits. For you it may work out that way. Or it may take more time. Given a choice, I'll visit an area at least half a dozen times before deciding, spending a fair amount of my time while I'm there with county street maps, driving slowly through residential and commercial areas, at all hours, until I know the area almost as well as the one where I live now. But if the relocation decision is one you pretty much feel you have to accept, two well-organized trips will help you make a good choice. Don't unpack everything, though, until you're sure you've made the best choice.

Career Change?

If you want to seriously consider a career change, you must be candid about what salable skills you have and what you are lacking. For instance: You've been an insurance salesman and now you want to become a newspaper editor? Chances are slim to nothing that you'll succeed in this kind of career change.

But: You've been an insurance salesman and you want to become a financial writer, and you've written and sold articles on financial subjects. Fine. Check out the possibilities for full-time employment. If you've been published, you at least know where to find out who hires financial writers and how much they're paid. Can you make enough at it to support yourself, and if necessary, your family? If not, can your spouse's job make up the difference?

Any career change has to be grounded in economic reality: yours and your new employer's. All you have to do is demonstrate how you can produce in a new job quickly enough. That's exceptionally hard to do, but not impossible, especially if you've been seriously planning for it. And in this situation, a salary cut may be justified if it will help you get into something you genuinely enjoy, or on a new career track with greater growth potential.

The problem is, many people have no idea what it is they like, and are uncertain what they are really best at. In fact, most people are like that. Few of us are as certain about anything as the guy who, from age seven on, knew he was going to be a lawyer. (And few of us, thank God, are that dull.)

But in this difficult time, you *need* to become certain. You need to resolve your doubts. If you don't, your recovery effort may lead you in unproductive directions. Someone who does something just because that's what he's always done, or because it was the best job offer he got after college will never impress anyone as being the dedicated and professional worker that the dullard attorney is.

If you don't have a high aptitude for what you are doing, your job performance will always be handicapped; you'll always be struggling. That may be one thing "average" performance ratings are telling you. Now is the time to pay for objective professional advice. Professional aptitude testing can range in scope from a $50 mail-in questionnaire to several hundred dollars' worth of written tests and psychological interviews. In mid-career, thinking about fundamental changes, there are far more wasteful ways to spend your money than on a good second opinion about yourself. You may in the end reject all the advice you have paid for, but by then you should have gained one important benefit: You should have resolved your doubts.

If you're really lucky, you are very good at what you enjoy doing most. If you're not, you have to consider one of life's great trade-offs: continuing in a career you have come to hate, or starting out to do what you love doing, even if it means a substantial and long-term pay cut. Some people can't bear the thought of taking a step down in pay, but some of the most contented, fulfilled people I know did just that.

In fact, you may reach the point where you will recognize the need to accept a cut, because you may come to realize you have no choice but to try something different. The career you have been following may simply have disappeared, and there are many reasons why this could happen. Competitive pressures may have forced organizational streamlinings; work you did that once was highly specialized and therefore valuable is being done by generalists; or services that were once in high demand became too expensive, and cheaper substitutes were found.

It's not pleasant to contemplate the possibility that your career may have disappeared in the mists of business history. But once you have accepted that reality, if you change your focus a bit, you may see opportunities you haven't noticed before, interests you can capitalize on, even if it means making a major lifestyle change. The change will be worthwhile if you see other offsetting advantages that will give you greater control: the opportunity for equity, or for more truly satisfying work in a job or in a business in which you have professional and competitive advantages, advantages that will insulate you from the changes making others obsolete.

The importance of being versatile in your career development can't be emphasized too strongly. This may seem difficult to do, with today's emphasis on specialized experience. But if you can get varied experience—working at different times in sales and engineering or in the same general profession, but in two different industries—your options will be broadened considerably. And the more options you have the more control you'll be able to exercise.

Career Planning: A Start

Career planning is like financial planning: you have to start doing it now. You have to prepare a plan that fits your circumstances and you must stick to it.

The kind of plan that I find of little use these days is the one that says, "Here's where I am now, and here's what I want to be doing 5 years from now . . . and 10 years." The business world has become so much more dynamic that so concrete a plan may be obsolete a year after it's written. Don't misunderstand—benchmarks are important. Far better, however, to benchmark skill development.

If that development is the key to your career plan, you will be able to adapt it to changes in the business environment you can't imagine now. From your experience, from your introspective analysis, and from the aptitude tests, you should have decided what career moves if any you need to make next to recover. Spend most of your time now on that work; keep that tight focus; don't daydream. But at appropriate times, when you've made significant progress toward your first objective or for a brief change of pace, start to think systematically about the future beyond your next job. These are the kinds of questions you should be thinking about:

- Can I take the skills I have now and apply them in other areas? If I can, how much new training will it take, how much time and expense will it involve, and will there be a real payoff in terms of increased income and broadened opportunities? How likely am I to succeed in the new areas? How do my aptitudes and preferences match up?

- Given the answers to the preceding questions, what are reasonable goals for one, two, three, and four years after recovery? Think carefully about time frames for your goals; review them every year and be prepared to revise them, but don't use that review as an excuse to keep pushing them back.

- What goals can I set that will take longer than four years to realize, yet at the same time will add to my options? Would giving myself an extra four. or five years give me a real start toward a completely new career (i.e., switching from medicine to law)? What are the costs in money and time? What's the likely payoff? At this early stage, what might be my chances of success? Would I like it? Love it?

- Write out all your plans in detail. Set priorities for developing options that will require major commitments of time to develop the requisite skills. Then prepare a more detailed one- and two-year operational plan that will specify the kinds of training you'll need first, the places you'll get it, when you'll start, how you'll pay for it, and the changes you'll have to make in your lifestyle to accommodate it.

Revise and update the plan annually, or whenever new inputs require it (you hate a particular course; or you've dicovered an interesting new possibility).

You're from the Government and You Want to Help Me?

If you're a government employee, at any level—local, county, state, or federal, but particularly the first three, you are probably thinking about job security, which is something you have never had to be concerned about before. There is more serious talk now about reducing government staffing levels than at any time since the Great Depression.

In addition to threatened or actual layoffs, there is unprecedented consideration being given to *privatization,* the turning over of entire government functions to private enterprises for what is presumably a more cost-effective delivery of services. Even if you are solidly entrenched in a civil service system and not at all threatened with the loss of your job, if there are significant layoffs elsewhere in your area, you may have to resort to *bumping*—displacing someone at a lower level— to keep working.

If any of these prospects disturb you, now is the prudent time to begin thinking about life in the private sector. Consider what will be necessary to make the transition.

The first problem you are going to encounter is the widespread notion that government workers, especially longtime employees, are slothful, are unwilling to work long, hard hours, and can't handle today's high-pressure work environments. You may not think this is fair, but that's the perception many potential employers have, and it presents you with a difficult problem to overcome.

To solve this problem, be honest with yourself, and try to appreciate what you are getting into. If you haven't worked outside government in many years, it'll be hard for you to comprehend just how intense the pressure can be. If you harbor any doubts about your ability to handle 50+ hour weeks and everything that comes with them, think about other options. Those would include nonprofit enterprises, foundations, and quasi-government operations such as state or local authorities.

If you're determined to make the transition, you can make your case to a private company in a number of ways. You can relate past experience in pressure situations, or a current part-time job in a competitive business, or, if you can be convincing, talk about your high energy level and your frustration with the slow pace of government work.

If you do get a job in the private sector, no matter what you've imagined, the required intensity level is going to surprise you. Don't act surprised. Act as though you thrive on pressure. Don't hesitate when you're asked to work on a weekend or give up evenings. You will either overcome any prejudice against former government types by your performance, or longingly start filling out civil service applications again.

Some government workers unfortunately do bring seriously inappropriate attitudes with them when they leave the public sector. In recent years most enterprises have become what they like to call "customer driven." They take pride in becoming more "market oriented," more sensitive to their customers' needs. Behind the rhetoric is a genuine concern: that the businesses that don't court their customers in every way possible—with prompt, friendly, courteous, attentive, responsive, and personable service—are going to be driven out of business.

Additional self-analysis is required to determine the degree to which you suffer from this attitude problem. It's not easy to come from a life where little attention is paid to customers' needs to one in which they are an obsession. It is a handicap you'll have to start overcoming from your first interview. Every way you communicate, from the way you speak to your body language, must convey your friendliness, sensitivity, and willingness to extend yourself.

Do you think you need practice? Try the tried-and-true route: comparable work on a part-time basis. The possibilities are limitless. Try working as a telephone customer service operator; an airline ticket counter agent; a bank teller; any place where unflagging courtesy under great pressure is essential. Such experience on your résumé will help you make the move you want, even if it takes more time and work than you had imagined.

Adapting your government skills to the private sector may be impossible, or it may turn out to be easier than you thought. If you worked for years in an arcane field such as grants administration, you may find that you have a great deal of catching up to do. But if you worked for a regulatory agency, you may find a high degree of similarity between what you've been doing on one side of the table and your private sector friends have been doing on the other side. A big difference you will notice immediately is the pace of work. You may do more on some days than you used to do in a week.

The point is, many solid professionals regularly make successful transitions from public employment to private enterprise. As with any job change, identifying and satisfying the needs of your new employer is the first requirement.

CHAPTER FOUR

Getting Organized

You are about to start on an endeavor which, if you do it right, will be one of the most satisfying experiences of your life. When you've completed it successfully, you will have developed an entirely new perspective on yourself and your work environment. You'll have acquired new skills and built your self-confidence to a level that can never again be undercut. From then on, you will have the control necessary to advance in accordance with your needs and interests.

No one likes to leave the comfortable womb of a nice job to go out alone into the world to find another job. But now you have no choice. The only choice you have in finding a new job and building a new career is whether you build carefully or haphazardly. The process involves several steps:

1. Deciding what it is you want to do—what your immediate objective is (this is covered in Chapter Three).

2. Developing that most important selling document, your résumé.

3. Organizing your job search.

4. Executing your job search.

5. Getting through the interviewing process.

6. Concluding final negotiations for your new job.

7. Staying in control after you have started a new job.

This chapter will get you started on your search and take you through the preparation of your résumé.

When you leave a job suddenly and unexpectedly, it is often difficult to focus on what it is you want to do next with your career. But after you have recovered from the shock of separation, that is exactly what you must focus on. You will not get very far if you don't. You won't even be able to start writing a résumé.

If you are going to use the time to consider other options to the career path you've been on, fine! The previous chapter showed you how. But do it systematically, and do it soon.

What options do you really have? You can quickly eliminate those that won't immediately provide your minimum acceptable level of income, or that require additional training or education that will be too time-consuming and expensive to acquire, or are in industries that have either stopped growing or are declining. The assumption from here on out is that you want to continue with what you've been doing, but have to consider a career change as one option.

Contrary to what some counselors may tell you, it is perfectly okay to try for more than one type of job, to have more than one objective. It will mean more work for you and require that you pay special attention to the organization of your multiple searches, but the end result may be much to your advantage—a truly satisfying career, and one that may not have been uppermost in your mind when you began your search.

The suggestion that you should consider two career options and have two distinct résumés for that purpose may not be easy to visualize. There are several ways it can be done; shortly we'll consider two of them. Before doing so, let's discuss why you may have to consider something other than the work you've been contentedly engaged in for the last several years.

It's important that, soon after leaving your job, you try to determine whether you'll be able to find another job in your chosen field within 60 days. If there are any negative signs, such as industrywide staffing reductions in your specialty, not just in your company, then you should start identifying a second option.

Or you may simply have another option that you believe has a good chance of working out for you. This won't be some frivolous notion of a dream job. It may not have evolved out of the career planning process outlined in Chapter Two, but you've gone through all the steps and come up with enough positive indicators to want to go ahead. That's great. In a climate of uncertainty, it could be one of the wisest actions you'll take.

It didn't turn out that way for a onetime neighbor of mine, but his experience ended positively nonetheless, and it shows how the two-track approach can work. For many years this man had worked as manager for several large manufacturers. In an era of specialists he had stayed a generalist. He wasn't a job-hopper, but he changed jobs regularly for promotions and for broader experience.

He became well known in his industry, and as a result he came to the attention of a large bank that wanted to expand the range of financial services it offered to companies in his industry. He wasn't what banks call "credit trained," but like most modern managers he would not have experienced the career growth he had without solid financial savvy. So when he was approached and made an attractive offer, the transition didn't intimidate him in any way. A productive new career of six years ensued, but as has happened so often lately, the bank got into deep trouble. There were many cutbacks, including his job.

His first choice was not a return to his former management work. He enjoyed the financing side of the business, but thought a lateral move within banking might be too risky. He had become expert at structuring financings and thought that experience could be made to pay off. He developed an excellent résumé, which showed how the structures he had put into place saved money and demonstrated his worth. He sent it to other financial institutions where that kind of capability was important (not necessarily where that kind of work was being done but where the capability could be *used*). Good headway was made, but high-quality job offers were not forthcoming. The kind of jobs that interested him required a more precise fit than he could offer. He eventually received feelers from a former competitor company in the industry he'd left. The feelers turned into an offer he couldn't refuse.

More recently, a longtime associate was terminated from a job she enjoyed, which paid her well. She concluded early on that finding a comparable job would be a long shot at best. She made the effort, professionally and enthusiastically, but paid most attention to two other options. One was in a closely related field, the other in a different area where perhaps only 50 percent of her recent experience was relevant and salable. Within the 60-day deadline she had set, she persuaded an enterprise that her 50 percent was worth a great deal. Not as much as she had been making, but there were other compensating factors.

Again, she pursued the other options smartly. She identified the precise needs she had to satisfy for each job, and in her résumé showed how her capabilities, though "nontraditional" could satisfy those needs.

The two-option approach, it should be noted, is probably not something you are going to get much help on from your outplacement counselor. They are best at getting you back to what you've been doing through a sharp focus on a continuation of your present career.

It is important, however, not to rush off in too many directions. If you do that you are likely to prolong your search unnecessarily. Few people can handle looking for more than two jobs at the same time. But it's a perverse truth of today's job market that not working on at least one other option simultaneously can prolong your search unnecessarily also.

The assumption here is that you have some good ideas about the two options that you intend to focus on. Those ideas you have to commit to paper, in the form of a short, specific statement of your career objectives. Whether or not you head up your résumé with this statement, it is important to develop it. Doing so will force you to clarify your thinking, to make decisions about what it is you want to do. Then you can start working on the résumé.

One of the first things I noticed when I started thinking about this book was the amount of information available on résumé writing. In one large bookstore I counted 14 titles on the subject. Two large suburban newspapers carried six classified ads for résumé-writing services. With all this good material readily available, the last thing I thought I'd have to discuss with any interested, intelligent reader was how to write an effective résumé. The era of the sloppily written, what-is-this-person-trying-to-tell-me résumé was long gone, I assumed.

But a spate of résumés that have crossed my desk recently convinced me my assumption was wrong. Even if this small sample does not represent a downward trend, the preparation and presentation of a résumé is so important to effective job changing that it is worth spending some time on here.

One rather extreme example says everything about the impact your résumé must make. A former human resources officer of a Fortune 500 company told me that when they run a help wanted ad in a major newspaper, the large number of responses they get dictates just how long they can spend reviewing each one: 30 seconds. If some things in your résumé don't grab the reader in that time, your chance for further consideration is gone.

If those seem like impossibly long odds, you're right. They are. And your chances of getting a job through a classified ad in any event are much less than by other methods. But if you don't make a serious effort to make an impact, your chances are nil. Our objective, then, is to prepare something that is going to open the door to the interviewer's office.

It's amazing how many of the résumés I receive are so bad that I'm tempted to put them in a file labeled, "Don't Hire These Poor Souls—Ever!" Examples: A covering letter of six short paragraphs, each led by the word "I"; a list of several job objectives, each requiring specific *and different* experience; and—many offenders here—covering letters that state job objectives completely different than those listed at the head of the résumés.

These deficiencies may be more obvious to me than they are to those who wrote the résumés, but this is not something you should treat as casually as these folks obviously did. The résumé and its covering letter is your calling card, and you have to make sure it gets your message across. You can't do that just by reading it back to yourself after you've prepared a first draft. You need second opinions, you need to look at examples of what others consider good résumés, and you need to take the time to do this part right.

To begin with, there are some points that have not been adequately covered elsewhere. *You need to prepare more than one résumé.* You may develop one standard résumé for use in your mass mailings for your prime objective, but you will need others for other purposes, which we'll discuss shortly. Also, the covering letter that must accompany every résumé is as important and in some respects more important than the résumé itself. Each covering letter must be tailored to the résumé it accompanies.

The reason you need multiple résumés is this: Every résumé is a "selling document," used to sell your accomplishments and abilities. That point can be restated in a way that makes its importance clearer to you. What you're really selling is your ability to do a job for someone, to satisfy a specific set of needs. And, because every potential employer will have different needs, it is important to tailor each résumé to those needs, to the greatest extent possible. This is easier said than done; how do you find out what those needs are? You have to do the best you can with what you have, even if all you have is a display ad from the newspaper.

When I'm working with a headhunter on a specific position, I try hard to write a special résumé just for that position, based on all the information I can glean from the headhunter. Although it's usually impossible to learn a great deal about an employer's needs from an ad, you can with a little hard work learn enough. It's easiest if you are not changing careers, just companies. Then you can prudently assume that a new job's requirements will be essentially the same as the old one's.

Take your clues where you find them. What requirements does an advertisement stress? The résumé you send in must emphasize how you'd satisfy them. What information can you get about the position's requirements from your network? It's not inconceivable that members of your network could provide you with insights which, incorporated into your résumé, give you a competitive edge. What information are you able to glean from talking directly to a human resources officer in the company you're applying to? Nothing, you will often find out. But occasionally, particularly if the competition for the slot is not especially fierce, you will find one who is willing to open up and help you. It never hurts to ask.

Two more points should be mentioned before we actually get into the structure of the résumé. First, only one résumé per position. Decide before you start writing what kind of job you're applying for (if you are not responding to an ad). If there is more than one type of job in the same company for which you feel qualified because of the range of your abilities and experience, write more than one résumé.

There's a good reason for this. Few things are more disconcerting to a potential employer than to pick up a résumé that has at its head under "Objective," "A position in the _____ industry in _____ or _____ or _____."

That shotgun approach may work—but rarely does. The reader is more likely to conclude that (a) you really haven't decided what you want to do, (b) you're a Jack (or Jill) of all trades and master of none, and (c) there's no way to tell from the welter of information presented what needs you think you can satisfy.

It's perfectly o.k., up to a point, to be undecided on a future career direction, but it's not o.k. to convey the uncertainty to others. What you must do is narrow your choices to a realistic few, and then prepare a résumé for each one as though that was the only one. A résumé can't be a multiple-choice exam for the reader. It's you who will fail if it is.

That sounds like an ironclad rule, doesn't it? Well, as I hope you're finding out, ironclad rules—those nice simple prescriptions found in many advice books—don't always hold up in the light of practical experience.

Are there times when it's appropriate for the objective at the head of your résumé to be vague or imprecise? Absolutely! It should never be vague, of course, when you're applying for a specific job. But there may be jobs out in the "hidden job market" (the market where jobs exist that aren't advertised) that you simply don't know about and don't know you're qualified for. Pursuing that possibility should be part of your job search.

Here's how. Begin by taking your standard résumé; change the objective at its head to read something like this: "A position that uses my experience in _____, and my capabilities, which include _____." This should be sent to a number of generalist headhunters (not the specialist firms who will be your main focus) accompanied by a covering letter that describes what you are trying to do. "I've been engaged in _____, and I've (accomplishments, capabilities); however, I'd like to explore other possibilities beyond those considered traditional for a professional with this background." This lets the recipient know why your objective is deliberately vague.

The probability of a payoff can't be considered high, but it has worked for me and I have been extremely pleased with the results. More than ever, it is worth trying. It is a shot in the dark, but nontraditional qualifications for any job have a better chance than ever of being considered, as many companies consider nontraditional approaches to doing business.

If the résumé conveys the substance of the contributions you can make to a company, it is the covering letter that must make the reader interested in your résumé. Never more than one page in length, it must *immediately* identify the specific position you are seeking. Then it must summarize the most important points in your résumé. It can't, because of the necessary space limitations, be a point-by-point recapitulation of your entire career. It instead has to contain what you think are the points of most interest to the recipient. Select several key capabilities and accomplishments from the résumé and present them, after the introduction, in a concise, logical sequence. The tone should be as professional as any business letter—no forced informalities, just clear, plain English. Let your accomplishments speak for themselves. Never send out a cover letter or a résumé after just one draft. Don't pretend that you are that exceptional person who is an excellent first-draft writer, because chances are you are not. The covering letter should always relate to the same kind of position, or job objective, as the résumé.

These are some of the fundamentals of résumé writing. So important; so easy to butcher. Remember:

- Keep it short. You will never get to first base with any employer if your résumé goes on for page after page. If your experience has all been in one area or with one company, one page may suffice. For most people, two pages is plenty. More isn't better.

- Be a brutal editor. Boil your prose down to its barest elements, to focus the reader's attention on the essentials of your accomplishments and capabilities.

- Don't get cute. Your résumé is from a professional to a professional. It is not a casual, friendly letter to an old acquaintance. Although you shouldn't be modest in describing your accomplishments, state them simply and matter-of-factly, without hyperbole.

- Stick to a chronological résumé. For each period of employment, describe briefly what your responsibilities were and, in more detail, what you accomplished. There was a trend a few years ago toward "situational résumés," which emphasized describing for each job, the "problems" you identified, the "actions" you took, and the "results" you produced. The idea was that this would give a potential employer a more well-rounded view of your problem-solving capabilities. A nice idea, but awkward and rather ineffective in practice.

- Quantify accomplishments. You have to. In dollars and cents to as great an extent as you can. This will emphasize your business acumen and establish you as a producer of results.

- Proofread. Again and again, to make sure that in the final draft that goes to the printer there are no misspellings, mistakes in grammar, or typographical errors. You can read your résumé over and over without finding a mistake, so be sure to let someone else proofread it as well.

- Use "action" verbs. A trendy little device, but a useful one, especially in a résumé that's tightly edited and aimed at making the maximum impact quickly. The résumé books have lists of these verbs. Using them properly can help get your message across while keeping it focused.

- Proofread it one more time, after it has come back from the printer. They have been known to make mistakes. Ask a friend to proofread it again.

Now the draft is written; this is a good time to compare it with some of the examples in résumé books. Checking through books with sample résumés may highlight any gross mistakes in your draft, but it can't tell you if it works. For that you need help. You need to try it out on friends. Ask some of them to consider what you've written as though they were prospective employers.

If you can, get the opinions of a department head and a staff (human resources) officer. Consider their comments carefully, incorporate those you think improve the résumé, and get the darn thing printed. There is no one best résumé, but there is one that works best for you. Later on, talk to some of those who've rejected you to see if the résumé was a factor. Fine-tune the résumé. Then move on to other things, such as deciding who to send the résumés to, and when.

Who Gets the Résumés?

The single most important thing you should have taken home from the office is your Rolodex file of professional contacts—names, addresses, and telephone numbers. Review every name on the list and put them into five categories: "call," "visit," "send letter," "send résumé," "forget about."

Don't discard the "forget about" pile. You aren't going to do anything with them now; they are your most casual, distant contacts. But in a few months if you haven't gotten a job, you may want to consider them again, as "desperation" contacts.

The other four categories of contacts are where you will begin your search, and, assuming the preparation of your résumé took Week 1 at the outplacement office, this is how you'll begin Week 2; this is how you'll organize and execute your job search. It is hard, frustrating work, because most of it involves what salespeople call "cold calling": calling on people you've never met, selling a product, yourself, they haven't expressed any previous interest in buying.

Almost immediately you are also going to start sending out

résumés in response to newspaper advertisements. Don't expect much from these ads, because the competition for advertised jobs is ferocious. Also, because of the time it takes to screen responses, arrange interviews, and select finalists, even a successful application may take many months—probably more time than you can afford to take. But you cannot risk not responding to ads, especially those in which you see a high degree of conformity between the stated job requirements and your capabilities.

You may have better success in responding to ads placed in trade or professional journals, especially if you work in a specialized occupation. That's because you probably already meet the minimum requirements for many of the jobs advertised, by the nature of your specialization. As with newspaper ads, however, the selection process can be drawn out.

You should respond to every ad with your résumé, and a covering letter that states why you can fill the requirements of the job advertised. Follow up all ads by telephone within two weeks to make sure your résumé has been received and to learn the hiring timetable. Then call in every other week until you're either invited for an interview or are told you're out of the running.

One level above the "forget about" category is the "send letter." You'll send letters to people who you've known more than casually but aren't close friends. You are asking for advice and help. Explain your situation, ask for advice on who you should be talking to—who has information about jobs, who's actually hiring. You don't at this time enclose a résumé, but you do follow up once, in about a week, on the phone, having stated your intention to do so in the letter. However, if the person to whom you're writing has in the past indicated any willingness to help in your career, enclose a few copies of your résumé and ask that they be circulated to interested parties. Again, follow up with a call in about a week.

After sending out some résumés and letters, don't sit around waiting for responses; get on the telephone. Your calls will go to anyone in your Rolodex you think can offer you serious help in your job search. These are from your "call" and "visit" list. These may not be your closest friends, but they should be good professional contacts.

Because your contact with them may have been intermittent, what you have to do now is "qualify" them. This means apprising them of your situation, and asking them for specific help: (1) Who's hiring? (2) Who are the key decision makers? (3) Do you know them? (4) What's the best way to contact them? (5) Can I use your name in a letter, or, even better, could you arrange a meeting? Asking for this degree of personal involvement is risky, however, and should only be attempted with your best contacts, those who have expressed a willingness to actively help you.

The more positive the answers are as you proceed through this list, the more important it is that you make personal visits to your contacts to solidify your relationships and signify their importance to you.

It's time now to see your closest professional friends. You'll be asking the same questions as above, but over a lunch you're buying, and after a more low-key lead-in question, such as, "What advice can you give me as to where I should focus my job search?"

Note one important thing about the letters you've sent out and calls you've made to this point: In no case have you asked directly for a job. This may seem needlessly coy and deferential, but it really isn't. Most people like to be helpful. If they like you at all, they will bend over backward to be of assistance. They'll be flattered you asked. But a direct job request puts them on the spot and makes them feel uncomfortable. No matter how desperate you get, you should never put anyone in that position; they will be of no future use to you. Besides, it won't be necessary to ask directly. The message is there, and if the line is open it will be received.

All the activities you've initiated, all the letters and résumés you've mailed, all the calls you've made, may have taken days or weeks to complete, depending on how lengthy a list of contacts you were able to accumulate.

Every call should include a request for additional people who can be contacted. This is an important way to generate new leads and sustain your search. You will run up against dead ends, but you should constantly be generating new contacts and new leads, until you start generating interviews and job offers.

Your objective, discussed more in the next section, should be to be employed within 60 days. That's an important objective, but you shouldn't panic if you don't make it. If you haven't begun to generate interviews in 60 days, though, you should reassess the elements of your search.

As you go about selling yourself over the phone and face-to-face, remember that you want to act at all times like a salesperson: alert, enthusiastic, relaxed. One of the new skills you will be acquiring is how to present yourself effectively even when you feel lousy. In your situation there may be days when you feel so depressed that you just can't fake it. If so, take that day off. Do other work related to your search, then take a few hours to do something completely different: anything that will refresh you and brighten your outlook.

Do It Now

You may be advised by an outplacement counselor that it will take three to six months or longer to find a new position, particularly if you are a highly paid professional. Hiring for professionals tends to be done at one time during the year, often in the first three months; hiring is slowest during the summer and at the very end of the year. So, you will be told, you have to be prepared to take the time necessary to find the right position.

In these times that is extraordinarily dangerous advice. It

may wind up taking six months, or longer, but you should do everything you can to see that it doesn't. *Your objective should be to be reemployed within 60 days of your last day at your old job.* I do not mean within 60 days of the day your severance package ends, because that could mean a lengthy gap in your actual professional employment. I mean 60 days after you have left work, no more.

That will not be easy to do. If you've been through this before, you know that it often takes 30 days just to get an interview arranged, and it can easily take two or more interviews per opening, and another 60 days may elapse before any job offers are made. And you certainly don't want to take the first job offered you, do you?

In fact, you may well want to. In today's work environment, there is only one criterion that should matter to you more than any other: compensation. While you certainly should try to get a raise, if you receive a new job offer with no more than a 10 percent cut from what you were making, GRAB IT! Why? Because the longer you are out of work, the more your reputation will be damaged, and the damage done increases rapidly after 60 days, and it is irreparable damage.

I know this isn't a majority view. Management recruiters may not agree and company personnel managers may be more understanding, but to the person on the line, who will have to make the ultimate hiring decision, you are damaged goods if you've been a beached whale for much more than a month.

If you've heard that view expressed, you know what they are saying: Nobody who is any good would take so long to relocate; you must have a major defect. They may be egregiously wrong in this view, they may have no knowledge of how long a 1990s job search takes, or may not want to take a chance. Either way you lose, and the longer you wait the more you lose.

Do not underestimate how serious your situation is. If

you can honestly conclude from contacts you make in the first 48 hours after you leave your old job that you will be able in perhaps 60 to 90 days to generate several attractive job offers, then you are a reasonably hot commodity in the job market and just maybe you can afford to be more patient than I'm suggesting you should be. But ask yourself this question: If the job market is as hot as I think it is after two days of making calls, why wasn't I aware of it when I was working? That is a question you should never have to ask again.

Is compensation the only important factor? Just about. While you probably shouldn't consider a cut more drastic than 10 percent until you've been in the market more than 60 days, a 10 percent cut may be acceptable if you gain other offsetting advantages, such as the opportunity to broaden your experience or a shot at more rapid promotions. And if you are changing careers, an even larger cut won't be fatal to your future.

If your next job truly was going to be your last one, then I'd argue more forcefully that you hold out longer for an offer that satisfies more of your objectives. But it's no longer safe to bet that it will be. Any new job, however good it may be, should be considered in part as a way station en route to one that's still better. A major objective is to stay employed with minimal interruptions at decently high salaries, not to satisfy every dream you've ever had.

On the other hand (there's always an "on the other hand," isn't there?), you should try to get the highest possible offer for a new job. Look at the math of the situation and you'll see why. If, in your eagerness to get back to work, you accept an offer that's $5,000 a year less than your new employer would be willing to offer if you negotiate hard, you haven't just lost $5,000 in one year. You've lost $5,000 every year as long as you stay there.

Persistence is rarely fatal when negotiating, as long as you're gracious and have a sense of when to stop pushing. Do not let your situation discourage you from asking for more. It is natural to be discouraged, and the longer you've been out, the more discouraged you may become. But when you're negotiating, you have to try to control those feelings and concentrate on selling yourself as though you were prime-quality goods—which you are!

Be aware of one possible handicap in your situation, however. Human resources people can act like vultures; when they know that you've been outplaced, they may try to place a ceiling on any offers you can be made, a ceiling that's several thousand dollars below what you might be offered if you were still employed.

Their job is to fill a slot at the lowest possible cost to their employer, and if they can do it in this nasty little way, they will do so and won't lose any sleep over it. In this situation there is no easy choice. Even if you feel compelled to accept a lowball offer, the fact that the tactic was used may embitter your relationships as long as you are there. If you then consider turning down the offer, you may worry when the next offer that's as good may come along.

Far too many people have an ideal situation that they feel they must satisfy the next time they change jobs, whether voluntarily or not: "This time I'm going to take the time to do it right." They want a shorter commute, or higher income plus performance bonuses, or more management responsibility, or more growth potential and more stability.

Fine. Start working toward that objective, when you start working regularly again, but don't expect to satisfy all your objectives in your next job. It won't happen that way, and you will hurt your search efforts if you are too picky. Do not worry that your commute has gone from 20 minutes to 90, or that the work is more demanding. Worry mainly about making a change as quickly as you can on at least the minimally acceptable terms.

The Myth of the Rear-Echelon Job:
Staff and Line

You should carefully consider the pros and cons of a career in staff work. By "staff" is meant the areas of personnel/human resources, advertising, marketing, internal auditing, government affairs, or similar functions where no direct customer contact or production is involved.

These functions are often the first to be reduced in any kind of layoff or in a merger. They are about the easiest functions in the world to duplicate, consolidate, or partly contract out, and the least visible. No company anywhere is known because of the quality of its personnel department. No decline in profit will ever be blamed on a downsizing of an internal audit staff. You are much safer in jobs dealing directly with clients, as in sales, or in production, which make a direct contribution to your company's income statement.

But suppose you are in personnel or public relations, and you like it? What can you do to reduce your risks? To begin with, recognize the risks. Recognize that you are always going to have a less secure job than someone who is producing on the line every day, bringing money directly into the coffers.

Next, realize that you are going to have to take certain steps to protect your future that the successful salesperson or supervisor on the shop floor doesn't have to be as concerned about. (Don't misunderstand: It's not all that hard for these types to become unemployed, either; it's just that they are in a relatively stronger position than you are.)

Learn what the competing companies are doing. In those companies, is the kind of work you do being expanded, reorganized, reduced, or eliminated? Evidence of expansion elsewhere should not necessarily make you feel more secure—it's possible that company is growing more rapidly than yours. But if you sense that your job might be in jeopardy, you obviously should take a closer look at the company that's expanding your function.

Next, evaluate the possibilities of a transfer within your company, to a different job. This is never easy, but it's a lot easier to do a one-step (new career path, same company) than a two-step (new career, new employer). And even if you like your staff job, the transition may be more practical than you think. You are a known quantity within your company, which is a tremendous advantage. You have come through the door, you've sold yourself to the people who make the hiring decisions, and you've been there for a few years; they are comfortable with you.

A transfer will almost certainly require the hard work of acquiring new skills, but if you haven't already developed contacts in the field in which you're interested, you're in the best position to do so. You can begin to acquire the new knowledge before you make your move to a new company. In such outside specialist companies, however, you are likely to find the competition more intense, the environment less secure, and the hours longer. And, to advance substantially, you may find that whatever your specialty is, the specialty you will have to get real good at is sales. In smaller entrepreneurial companies, the ability to consistently bring in profitable business determines more than anything else how long you'll be kept on, and at what level.

Terminated Twice

A problem encountered by increasing numbers in the job market is that they have been terminated involuntarily at least twice. Are you one of them? If so, I have bad news and good news for you. The bad news is, you have special problems. The good news is, they aren't crippling problems; I've known too many dynamic, successful people who overcame similar handicaps to believe that they are.

You are, you will have to admit, still in the minority. The second time leaving a job is not your decision, you should stop until you've figured out—honestly—what went wrong. I hate to come down on you at a difficult time, but there's a fair chance you're repeating one or more serious mistakes. They may be more mistakes of omission than commission, but that doesn't make them any less serious.

Review every point in Chapters One and Two. What did you miss? Was it just your bad luck to hook up with two companies in a row that were going down the tubes? Did you have any inkling of their condition before you hired on? Why not? Have you been accepting jobs at which you have no chance of excelling? Why? Do you know what you do best? Do you enjoy it? Are you working at it? Is there anything at all about you that offends people? Can you find out?

You would be unwise to activate a search for the third job until you have identified likely causes of your multiple terminations, and decided on a plan of corrective action. List the causes and keep the list. Refer to it whenever you sense you might be backsliding.

None of it was your fault? No way? I can accept that. Some things are beyond anyone's control—but not many. The objective of trying to find out where the faults lie is not to fix blame or depress you, but to help you see yourself as others see you. If that picture isn't good enough for today's job markets, then I'm certain you will want to make changes.

When those questions have been settled, activate your job search; lets's get this recovery on the road. What do you have to do differently? First, never think of yourself as a two-time loser. You are not a felon, just released from a long stretch in the Big House! Never mention it unless others do. Think about it: How is a prospective employer going to find out that you have been terminated twice? Your former employers shouldn't tell on you—all they should give is the dates of your employment.

In anticipation of any questions as to why you left previous positions, always be prepared to discuss what you know about the requirements of this job, and how you can meet them. That's right—don't look back, don't be defensive! It happened, you say. Next question. What can I do for you? That's what I'm here to discuss!

CHAPTER FIVE

Your Friend(?) the Headhunter

No single action you can take will do more to expedite your recovery than making effective use of management recruiters or "headhunters." They will be able to open more doors for you more quickly than you could ever do yourself. They can provide valuable information on job-market conditions, help you sharpen your presentation skills, steer you away from blind alleys, and provide timely, helpful feedback on interviews; and none of this will cost you a cent.

Of course not all headhunters will be so helpful. Some will be insufferable snobs who seem to be most concerned about catching infectious diseases from people with whom they come in contact. Others will be insensitive hustlers who simply want to place you in a job, any job, and quickly, so that they can earn a fee. Still others will be outright incompetents; professionals cut from other jobs without any special aptitude for matching people and positions. Most, you will find, are better than that. If you meet them halfway and convince them that you are both flexible and have something to bring to the table, they will work with you and for you.

A quick turnoff for headhunters is the job-seeker who is totally inflexible in his or her demands. The next job has to feature A, B, C, D, and E, and none of these points is negotiable. Welcome to the 1990s—everything is negotiable. Another nuisance is the overreacher, the job-hunting professional who has too little appreciation of how little he can actually offer. If your self-assessment hasn't provided these insights, a 20-minute conversation with a good headhunter will, and if you then can't shift down to more realistic expectations, you will find the headhunter turning his attention to other things.

Assuming you come across as both flexible and realistic in your first meeting, a headhunter then will want a résumé and references. He may ask you to revise the résumé to suit his needs. No matter how good the headhunter's reputation, you still want to exercise a degree of control over the distribution of your résumé. It's reasonable to ask that you be told who the résumé is being sent to. You have a veto power here, but it should be exercised only in extreme cases where you would never consider working for the company the résumé is to be sent to. Exercise the power too often and you'll find that fewer are being sent.

When employed, never release the names of references until you've entered into final negotiations for a job. When you are not working that rule doesn't hold. Some—not all—headhunters will want references right away, so they can check you out. It's likely that all they know about you at this juncture is what you've told them, and that may not be enough. They may feel it's important to get a more rounded appraisal of you as a person and a professional. Don't let this be a sticking point. Be prepared to provide the names of three or four absolutely trustworthy references, who know your situation and have agreed to act as general references.

There are basically two kinds of headhunters, contingency and retainer firms. A contingency firm learns of a vacancy and contacts the person responsible for filling it, who agrees to pay the firm a commission if, and only if, one of the firm's candidates is selected to fill the vacancy. This particular head-hunter may have similar arrangements with several other firms. This is the type you should expend most of your effort on. A retainer firm is selected by a company with a vacancy to be its sole agent in identifying, screening, and presenting candidates to fill the vacancy. The firm is paid whether or not a candidate is finally selected. Some firms handle both kinds of assignments.

When you're employed and you want to change jobs, a disadvantage of working with a contingency firm is that some of them may "shotgun" your résumé around the job market without your prior consent, greatly reducing your chances of conducting a confidential job search.

Even if you've been out of work for an extended period, you should still try to avoid having your résumé shopped indiscriminately. Few things will harm your chances in job hunting more than having the appearance of pawed-over stale fruit in the market.

Here is an idea of how you may be treated by a contingency firm of uncertain quality.

"Good morning, is this Richard Dudgeon? Yes, Dick, thank you for taking the time to talk with me. Dick, my name is Frank Overbyte and I'm with Huskster & Finagle, management recruiters. Dick, we're aware that you specialize in lamp design with Brigadier Electric, and I wonder if you could help me."

To the inexperienced, that initial gambit is a simple, effective grabber. Your response is predictable:

"Sure, what did you have in mind?"

Here it comes . . .

"We're looking for people in your specialty who might be interested in making a career change, and we wonder if you know of anyone in your company who might be in that situation."

"Not offhand."

You didn't get the message. Here it comes again:

"Rich, have you given any thought at all to exploring a change?"

You always want to come across as Joe Cool, so you answer that you are willing to "explore" anything.

The next thing you know you are slipping away on your lunch hour to meet Mr. Overbyte. His offices are unpretentious, not exactly like the quarters you'd one day like to occupy yourself, but what does impress you is Overbyte's interest in you. At this point you are doing almost all the talking, about yourself.

After 15 minutes of this, Overbyte says, "Dick, those are quite impressive credentials. With your permission, of course, and in complete confidence, we'd like to present them to one of our clients."

"Who might that be?"

"Well, as a rule I don't like to get that specific until I'm satisfied that there is some mutual interest."

"Oh."

"Dick, for you to consider a move, you mentioned you made last year 40 thou with bonus, for you to move, what would it take?"

You are hooked now. This could be the opportunity of a lifetime.

"Well, the total job environment is the most important thing to me, but I'd be interested at the 55 level."

Now you have just asked for a 38 percent increase, but Overbyte doesn't blink. He obviously recognizes you for what you are: a hidden treasure, an undervalued asset.

"All right, Richard, let us get to work. These things always take time, but we will get back to you."

"When might that be?"

"If you haven't heard from me in two weeks, why don't you check in?"

Three weeks pass and nothing has happened, and Mr. Overbyte's secretary says he is away on a business trip. A week after that, he gets back to you.

"Rich, I've spoken with them, they are interested, but the key guy, the guy you have to see, is right in the middle of his annual budget review, and he's not going to be in a position to do anything for 30 days or so."

Thirty days become three months, and unless your porch light is completely disconnected, you begin to realize there is nothing there.

Of course, Mr. Overbyte is not working for you, and he has no clients. What he does have is some knowledge of the way most businesses operate. Most businesses have set budgets for personnel, but they may also have unanticipated personnel needs. Overbyte is betting that, without any prior knowledge of a specific opening, he can come across one and fill it with a warm body. That will happen maybe one time out of a hundred, but he knows that if he makes enough cold calls, he will generate enough commissions to pay his rent.

There is no reason why he should take any special interest in you. If he does not get a reasonably quick positive response to your résumé, he may circulate it to other possible employers, even though you've told him not to.

That is why you should not work with an Overbyte while you're employed, because your chances of success are as remote as his. And the risks to you are great, because it is so easy for word to get back to your present employer that you are looking for a new job. Employed or unemployed, my limit on contingency headhunters is 45 days. If they can't at least set up real interviews 45 days after they've received your résumé, try another firm. A good headhunter will get on the phone to read the highlights of your résumé to his contacts soon after he gets it. That way it's sometimes possible to get interviews set up in a week or 10 days.

But you want to establish good contacts with headhunters, because you never know when you'll need one, right? Not really. Nobody has a long-term working relationship with a headhunter as a source of jobs. If it seems like one is trying to cultivate a relationship with you, it's only because you're seen as a source of information about what's going on in your company, a source of other "clients."

When you're unemployed, the situation changes. Confidentiality becomes much less important. You want people to know you're available. Then you have to separate the good contingency headhunters from the mediocre ones. The following example of a retainer firm on assignment is generally applicable to contingency firms, too. The beginning of your relationship will be different—you are contacting them—but their modus operandi should be similar.

The opening gambit of a headhunter on a mission, with an assignment, should be much more specific, something like this: "Mr. Dudgeon, we've been retained by a major company in your field to fill a position in kumquat testing. It's an existing position with room to grow in, and we know you're a testing specialist. If you're interested, I'd like to meet with you to get better acquainted." What you need to hear, of course, is that the headhunter is on retainer to fill a specific slot. That's no assurance, unfortunately, that if you take the bait, what follows will in any way advance your career. So it pays, during that first conversation, to get specifics. Ask the caller who referred you to him. Don't expect him to give you a name, but he should give you a plausible explanation, such as, "Our client was impressed by that technical article you wrote last summer and told us to be sure we included you in our search." Or, "You're well known in this area," and he'll mention some things about you that have appeared in the trade press.

Next get the details: a job description, expected experience level, general salary range, and any special requirements, such as relocation.

If you really think you are unqualified in any area the recruiter has mentioned as being important, express your reservation up front. Express it, but don't belabor it. State it as a legitimate concern, and let the recruiter make the judgment in responding. Should you do this over the telephone, during your first contact? It depends. If the qualification is fundamental, as for a doctorate he may mistakenly think you have, why waste anyone's time? But if the area is more gray, as with lack of experience, wait until you meet face-to-face. Then, if the position really interests you but your concern remains, talk about it in terms of how other relevant experience you have can more than compensate. Sell the idea of substituting what you have for what they say they want. If the recruiter is not buying, you should be shot down graciously, but completely: "Nah, I'm sorry, Mr. D., but there's no budging on that amount of experience. The requirements for the short list are for at least that level." But at least you tried.

Then, set a definite time limit on being interviewed by the headhunter's clients. A competent headhunter working on a real assignment will not string you along. Anything from, "you're out of the running" to "they've looked over the field, and they're going to leave the slot vacant for now" tells you it's over. Explanations of delays in scheduling interviews are reasonable, up to a point. Beyond that, it's more evasion, which you don't have to tolerate.

To maintain your credibility, set a cutoff date. Somewhere around 30 to 45 days after the first meeting at which you handed over your résumé, if you haven't even been scheduled for a screening interview, you should say, "Look, this is not developing along the lines we both hoped it might. I'd like my name withdrawn from consideration. Maybe next time." You don't have to be any more specific than that. Could your impatience in such situations destroy you? Not unless you ignore genuine and specific reasons for delays: "They want to fill another position first, they're making a final selection in the next 30 days, then they'll resume this search." That sort of continuation move is plausible—once.

Never, ever let the circulation of your résumé get out of control. The headhunter should tell you in advance who she's sending your résumé to: company and individual. This should be done only after she's described your qualifications in detail to the prospective employer without mentioning your name, and they have expressed enough interest to ask for a résumé. Anyone who won't agree to that procedure should not be given a résumé to begin with.

I've gotten to the point in dealing with contingency head-hunters where I insist on tailoring my résumé directly for each client. I give the headhunter a one-page résumé that highlights my career but does not provide a potential employer with enough information to make a hiring decision. It is enough for them to reject me out of hand, or ask for more. That's when I want to take over. I tell the headhunter, "Tell me the name of the company; I'll research them and their industry if I don't know them well now, and mold my résumé into a real selling document." Some good headhunters see the advantage to this approach, but many do not. It comes down to a question of who is in control.

The most important concern in starting out on a relationship with a headhunter is compatability. Don't let age or experience differentials put you off. I've seen people with virtually identical backgrounds take an instant dislike to each other, and I've seen odd couples develop an instant rapport that led to a quick and successful ending to the job search. A comfortable compatability may lessen the extent to which you have to be concerned about issues of control, but it doesn't eliminate it.

Controlling the situation is the key to success with head-hunters. Make sure there is a real job and a real intention to fill it. Recognize, though, that the best headhunters can be frustrated by fickle managers who change their mind about the job long after the headhunter has begun to work.

Of course, if you've been outplaced, you have to take a more activist approach. You first have to reach out to the retainer firms. Good luck. The retainer firms, they would have you believe, would be reaching out to you if you were worth including in one of their searches. They would know of you through their "data bank." "All right, send us a résumé, and we'll put it in the bank, and check back with us in 30 days and we'll let you know if there might be a match with anything we're working on." If you haven't been invited for an interview after 30 days, move on to other things.

Secrecy and confidentiality are no longer top concerns, right? Right. You don't care who is sent your résumé, right? Wrong. It's more important than ever that you identify contingency firms with real experience in your field, who are willing to work with you to find a fit. A lazy, marginally competent headhunter can still hurt you because in sending out résumés for slots for which you're plainly not qualified, your name will be negatively linked to this loser's.

Keep informed about what's being done or not done with your résumé. Every potential opening that the recruiter thinks is worth a résumé should be discussed with you. Ask how he found out about it—through personal contacts, or is he just using a clipping service from the classified ads of the Sunday paper?

Contingency firms really can help unemployed people find jobs. They can shorten the time it takes, even if they can't make the competition any less intense. Most don't have the snobbish attitude of retainer firms, and some may have been in your position. They are one more track you have to keep working.

Assume now that you have survived the headhunter's initial screening. Your résumé has been discussed in depth, your personal interests have been explored, you've been told the name of the client company and what the position is, and perhaps you've been invited to outline, preliminarily, your views on how you'd fill the position.

You are now scheduled for interviews with the people with whom you'd be working. (For a discussion of the interviewing process, see Chapter Six.) The objective here is to help you maintain control of your relationship with the headhunter, while advancing your chances of getting an offer.

The first thing to keep in mind is that you are not yet the

Anointed One; you are just one of a number of candidates the headhunter is showing to the client. You should expect to be told something about the interests and concerns of the people you'll be seeing; the headhunter should want all prospects to be at their best. You should also be told, at this stage, what the rest of the process will be: "All candidates will be interviewed this week. They may invite one or more of you back for second interviews, probably within the next two weeks, but one or more of you may be dropped from consideration after the first interview. If that's you, we'll let you know as soon as we know, and we'll also tell you what the client liked as well as what they weren't pleased with.

"Within a week after the second interviews, the client will narrow it down to one candidate and start negotiating. So when we call you that week, it will be either to tell you that you're out of the picture or that they'd like to have you as a colleague."

Has anybody out there ever worked with a headhunter who was so completely communicative? There are a few of them around. The communication just described is close to ideal in an area that is critically important to you: feedback. You just have to have it to keep on top of what is happening as you head down what may be the homestretch. If you don't, you may lack critical information you need to make decisions as you jockey for position among the finalists.

A good headhunter will report on your first interview without being asked. One distinction between a pro and a bush leaguer is how quick, candid, and thorough the postmortem is. A headhunter who strings you along when you are no longer under consideration is unfair, but it is often done for selfish reasons: to keep you in reserve in case negotiations with the higher choices fall through.

You must, at each stage, find out where you stand if you have any doubts. One sure warning sign is a long lag between a first interview you've been told went well, and the scheduling of a second interview. That could mean another candidate's already been back in and is in negotiations. Ask the headhunter if that is what's happening. A no answer should prompt your inquiry about the changed scheduling of the next interview. An evasive answer confronts you with a decision. In making it, do not burn any bridges (except in the case of the unusually inept performance that we'll discuss shortly).

You may want to say something like this: "Look, I sense, and you're not contradicting me on this, that they feel more comfortable with another candidate. So let me clear the decks and withdraw. I enjoyed working with you; let's keep in touch." Short, simple, and gracious. Should you respond in this way if you're unemployed? Probably not. You have more to gain than lose by being patient. But a fast-track, high-performing pro in a solid situation has the luxury of going with his or her instincts. Confirm your decision to withdraw from consideration in writing; and by all means, if you hit it off well, send a similar note to the senior person you met at the client's.

Keeping in contact with a potential client increases the possibility that a future job offer may be forthcoming. That's because in some cases, there isn't a clear number one and number two, but rather one candidate who best fits the client's special needs at that time. Many things can happen to suddenly change the situation and bring you right back into the picture. The successful candidate simply may not work out.

Occasionally there are incompatibilities that escape notice in the best screening processes, that become intolerable under the stress of the job. If that happens, some companies will simply decide to cut the knot quickly, rather than "try to work things out." It's also possible that a major change in a company's market environment may change their thinking and make you a more attractive candidate than you were initially.

But such uncertainties do not mean you have to tolerate what is plainly jerking around by a headhunter. Here's an example. Recently several people were contacted by a well-known management recruiting firm. All were invited in for lengthy screening interviews; four were selected as finalists for a position that was described in appropriate detail. Of the four, three were working and one was "between jobs."

The selection process as explained to them was straightforward: After a half day of interviews with senior managers, one, two, or all of the candidates would within 30 days be invited back for a day of sessions with all the middle managers who would be their colleagues. Within two weeks after the conclusion of those interviews, an offer would be made to one of the candidates.

Forty-eight hours after the first interview, one candidate called the headhunter for feedback. "They liked you," he was told. "The list is now down to three but you made a favorable impression. We'll get back to you on the next interview."

About 10 days later, this candidate was called by a close friend in another company who knew he was considering a move, but did not know that he'd been put into a selection process by this headhunter. "Hey, let me know if this interests you. I was contacted [by the headhunter!] about a position at _____. I told them I wasn't interested, but that I'd check around. Are you?" The careful response was, "How close is the company to making a decision?" His friend replied, "I can't tell. The headhunter said they'd sent one batch of possibilities in to see the client, but the client wanted to see what else was out there."

The candidate ended the conversation by saying he probably wasn't interested. Then he became furious! He called the headhunter immediately; "What's going on? Why wasn't I contacted?" The answer was almost unbelievably blasé. "We don't think anything has really changed," he was told. "We did a thorough search the first time. We're making calls because we're obliged to, so sit tight. You'll be hearing from us."

This person thought it over for a week, then sent this note to the most senior manager he'd been interviewed by, with a copy to the headhunter.

Dear Ms. Marmoset:
I was interested to learn that there's been a delay in your hiring plans. The reasons for the delay as I understand

them have to do with your desire for a good "fit" between candidate and position. That's always my first concern, too. And since that compatibility wasn't clearly felt by you and your colleagues after our meetings, I'm withdrawing from consideration at this time.

This letter was sent for two perfectly valid reasons: First, unlike the headhunter, he took the client at her word. She may not have known what she wanted, but she knew what she didn't like. He accepted the reality of the situation—that the odds of his being made an offer were slim, and he wanted to get out in the most professional manner possible. Second, he lost all respect for the headhunter and his firm. They had not leveled with him and should have offered him the opportunity to withdraw. He felt obliged to take matters into his own hands.

He hasn't heard any more from the firm, and doesn't want to; but he did hear subsequent details from other sources. No new names were added to the list. After about 60 days, the two remaining candidates were invited back for the "final" interviews. Guess what they were told not long afterward? The client wants to see a new group of candidates! This gets better. None from the new list turned out to be acceptable, either. Almost nine months later, the position still hadn't been filled.

This was an unusual combination of a client that didn't have its act together and an amateurish, if not unethical, management recruiter. In these circumstances, the letter to Ms. Marmoset was entirely appropriate. But the others who hung in there to the end weren't wrong; their responses (sitting tight) were conditioned by their assessment of their situations.

Don't let any of this discourage you. Active cultivation of headhunters is one of the most important parts of your recovery strategy. What I hope to have done here is equip you to work with them effectively, professionally, and with your eyes wide open.

CHAPTER SIX

Making It Through Interviews

If you have been able to work well with the many headhunters you have now contacted, interviews should begin to come along at regular intervals. Before scheduling any interviews, read as much about interviewing techniques and negotiating as you can. As with résumés, there are good books available that cover interviewing techniques, and you should borrow or buy a few that seem to emphasize the areas you're weakest in.

From the perspective of one who has conducted dozens of interviews and been on many, the most important elements of interviewing are the most basic. Interviews are naturally stressful situations, and many otherwise competent professionals do poorly on interviews because they can't handle the stress. After all your preparation, you must appear relaxed when you arrive to be interviewed. But first, you must understand the important basics. That's what this chapter will concentrate on.

It's useful to separate interviews into two types: "screening" and "hiring." You have to pass the first to get to the second. A screening interview is usually conducted by someone with personnel responsibilities, if not by a human resources specialist. The interviewer may know little about the special professional skills that are the most important part of the job, but they will be skilled in the kind of questioning needed to flesh out the picture of you that is presented by your résumé. For example, they'll ask for additional information on experience you claim to have that the screener has been told is an important part of the job description. They may not know how to interpret all your answers, but they'll note what you say and notice if you sound tentative or unsure of yourself. They'll notice, too, how you present yourself: your directness, manners, warmth, graciousness, humor, curiosity, articulateness, and general intelligence.

Use this interview to find out as much as you can about the company, its culture and policies, the department you'd be assigned to, the people you'd be working with, and the job. Leaven your questions with facts you've uncovered in your pre-interview research. Don't ask about the salary or any other matters related to the "compensation package," such as fringe benefits. It's much too soon for such questions. But, it's not too soon to ask, after you've discussed the position for which you're applying, about the career path or track. In other words, what positions can you hope to advance to, what's required, and how long does it take? In your early interviews, touch briefly on this point, but do mention it, because it's important. We'll talk more about why it's important shortly.

Somewhere in the process you may be asked to take psychological tests. These might consist solely of timed, written tests or they may be combined with an interview with a Ph.D. psychologist. The purpose of the tests is to find out if you fit their "profile," if you have the kind of personality that's compatible with what they perceive to be their culture. These sessions can be grueling pressure situations that take up the better part of a day.

Does the prospect of having someone probe around inside your head bother you? There are good reasons for taking a hike when you're told that these tests are next on the agenda. Some people consider the tests an unnecessary invasion of privacy. They view employment as a working relationship, not a marriage. Indeed, some of the questions are personal and they can be tricky. You may, for instance, be asked about your family relationships and your personal life, and you may be asked the same question in different ways at different places in the tests.

I can't advise you to take a philosophical stand against such tests when you're confronted with the choice. Unless you're financially independent, you'll want to consider other factors before deciding. How attractive do all the other elements of the possible job seem to you? How long have you been out of work? Do you like the people? What are your other prospects?

I have a pragmatic objection to psychological tests. From every interview I've been on, I've tried to get feedback, and I'd love to have a professional perspective on the view from inside my skull, but I've never been able to get the psychologists to tell me anything about the tests I participated in. I resent that; it's too one-sided.

After the testing you'll move on to meeting with the people you will actually be working for. The emphasis will be on your professionalism; experience, knowledge, judgment. If you ever had a penchant for hyperbole, now it must be restrained. Nothing will destroy your chances faster than spouting baloney. The safest assumption you can make about these interviews is that everybody you'll see will know more than you do.

Expect that your knowledge in areas in which you claim to have expertise will be explored in depth, but don't expect to get much reaction to what you say. Few interviewers are so impolite as to respond with, "Boy, that was a dumb answer. How did you get to be where you were? We wouldn't hire you for our mail room."

It's entirely proper to ask about the levels of expertise that are expected so that you can feel reasonably comfortable that you aren't getting in over your head. In return, you may be asked "stretching" questions—questions designed to determine how thoroughly into your profession you are, and how much behind the normal boundaries of your profession your interests took you; how much you were willing to stretch the limits of your knowledge.

Changes of pace will come in the form of inquiries into your life away from the job. These won't be the kinds of probes you get on psychological tests, just normal questions about your hobbies, community activities, and other interests.

But this interview presents you with one of your best opportunities to determine whether you are likely to succeed in the job if it is offered to you. You cannot be passive in this interview; you must explore, by asking your own questions, the dimensions of the job. You have to learn, by relating examples based on your knowledge and experience. And, by considering the reactions to what you say, how your prospective superiors expect to see the job performed. In this sense, you have to do what many books tell you to do, "take charge" of the interview, by steering it in the direction you want to take it, to the conclusion that you're the one who should be hired.

You should be cautious, however, because it is easy to overdo the similarities between selling a product or service and selling yourself. In the case of the former, the sale is all that counts. When it comes to selling yourself, and you're out of work, of course, you want to be sold—but to the right buyer. That's an important distinction.

In the interviews, particularly your meetings with the people you'll be working with, you have to ask yourself, "Do I want to be bought by these people?" It is therefore critically important for you to find out as much about them as they are trying to find out about you. Not just their professional perspectives, but their other dimensions as well. What are their interests aside from work? Can you relate to those interests? Do you think you'll be able to relate to them effectively when the subject is something other than the job at hand?

If you have reservations, try to get additional information from third parties who may know the people you're interviewing with. You may get additional information in this way that will make your reservations go away, or you may learn things that will heighten your concerns. In that case, you'll have to decide whether you'll have to justify taking a chance on a job that may turn out to be more of a short-term situation than you'd like.

Sometimes it's impossible to get any independent verification of the impressions you're forming about key people in your interviews. That can happen when those people are new to the company or have come to their jobs from some other field. I was in that situation several years ago. The man I spent most of my time interviewing with, and with whom I ultimately wound up working, was unfailingly polite and low key in all our meetings before I was hired. That impressed me, but because he had been an independent consultant for the preceding 10 years, I was unable to locate anyone who could tell me firsthand what he was like to work with, whether his good manners were genuine or an act.

It turned out to be an act all right, the act of a Dr. Jekyll and Mr. Hyde. What I saw most after I started work was a martinet with a hair-trigger temper who was an absolute "control freak" and who treated his subordinates shabbily and his superiors with kid gloves. He could not conceal this contradictory behavior forever, and eventually he was treated very badly by senior management. His behavior mellowed thereafter, but I was never able to be completely comfortable working with him.

Surviving an interview is somewhat like running a gauntlet; you can get tripped up and hurt badly at almost any point, from start to finish. So you need to understand what's important in an interview and to an interviewer. These points are paramount:

Arrive on time. Precisely on time. No earlier than five minutes before the appointment, and not one minute late. It's surprising how many "professionals" show up, and insist on being announced, 20 to 30 minutes early. That's counterproductive, because it's an implied imposition on the interviewer's time. You may not have anything better to do with your time, but they sure do.

For reasons beyond your control, you may arrive late. When you know you're going to be late, don't panic! You'll blow the interview completely if you come across as a nervous wreck. If possible, call ahead to explain the delay. Ask for a later appointment on another date. Then relax and regain control of yourself.

Think about how you look. Different industries, even different companies within an industry have different standards of dress. You want to fit in with everyone else in the office, and if you can't take the time to check that out in advance, the rule to follow is this: Woman or man, the "neat" look is in and is going to be in for a long time. When in doubt, err on the conservative side. For men this means a suit; for women, a suit or a dress.

Looking reasonably normal (conformist), you proceed from the office door to the interviewer's desk and you shake hands; if you hand over a dead, limp fish, you're off on the wrong foot. You don't want to crack knuckles, but you do want to convey sincerity with a firm grip. And while you're doing that, establish eye contact and smile. The eye contact is critical. If it's not made, you'll come across about as sincere as a career congressman. Also, practice smiling, seriously. A friend of mine thought for a long time that he had a nice warm smile, but until he was told it looked more like a smirk, he didn't realize he was smiling with only one side of his mouth. Check yours out in a mirror.

You're invited to sit down, and a good interviewer does a couple of things out of common courtesy that should put you at ease and make it easier for you to perform at your best. First, you're introduced to the second interviewer, Janet Smith, and informed that she'll be participating in the interview. That's because the first interviewer wants to observe closely how you react to others, when he's not concentrating on asking you questions. This is common. Second, the interviewer should tell the secretary to hold *all* calls. An interview is a serious business for everyone, and should not be interrupted. If you are talking with people who have authoritative responsibilities, however, repeated interruptions may be unavoidable, but that doesn't make them any less distracting. I advise you to stay loose in such situations, even though you may be tempted to get up and leave after the third or fourth phone call or walk-in visitor. It's extremely difficult to sell yourself under these circumstances, but before you make a move you may later regret, try conveying your concern by a facial expression of exasperation. After the sixth interruption in half an hour, for example, you should politely inquire if another time might be better for the interviewer.

Far less common are "gang" interviews, where you're sitting on one side of a table and several others are across from you, firing questions at you as if you were under cross-examination in a courtroom. These ordeals can go on for hours, and can be incredibly stressful. You can be asked a question, interrupted by someone other than the questioner as you attempt to answer, and your answers can be criticized and derided. You can be exposed to ridicule, patronizing put-downs, and other rude behavior, such as an interviewer yawning in your face just after asking you a question. These are not the usual kinds of interviews most people experience. Once you find yourself in one, you must decide on the spot whether to proceed or cut it off.

Now the toughest part begins. You have to open your mouth and speak, intelligently and coherently. If you were a "C" student in English all the way through school, you may now be stepping close to the landmines. But if you listen to the questions and think about your responses before answering, you need not sound as erudite as William F. Buckley to impress the interviewers.

In speaking, *never use the phrase, "you know,"* as in, "I

graduated from, you know, Harvard in 1980," or "I was working as, you know (pause), a nuclear physicist . . ." Repeated
use of that one phrase drops you way down, if it does not
eliminate you.

Two other bad habits should be expunged from your speech
if you are afflicted with them. "Like" is as irritating to many
as "you know," as in, "I spent my senior year at, like, the
Sorbonne, in, like, you know, Paris?" And ending what should
be declarative sentences with question marks may be considered a relatively minor concern. But it's not professional, particularly if it's your normal pattern of speech, rather than a
device that's used occasionally to emphasize an important
point.

If these habits present problems to you, find a remedial
speech class or work the problems through with a speech
therapist. The improvements will help you in interviews and
will complement your other skills after you've returned to
work.

Next, nerves. You're expected to be nervous, so a little stut-
tering and uncertainty at first isn't disastrous. But however nervous you are, it's expected that you'll have a clear idea of what
you're there for: *you are selling yourself.* That means that as the
interview goes on, you'll ask questions to find out what interests the interviewers—in the salesperson's term, what their
"hot buttons" are. You must respond appropriately, learning
from your questions what their needs are; talking about how
you can satisfy them—and how you've satisfied similar needs
in other situations. That's the main reason for your interview,
and you must remain focused on it.

If you're concerned about your anxiety, ask your doctor if
there's anything you can take before an interview that will
ease your tension. I won't get specific here, but I've used
certain nonprescription formulations without harmful side effects. It is very important to appear calm, because a calm,
relaxed, and assured manner implies confidence, a quality you
must convey.

You cannot appear in an interview as a desperate supplicant, or as a world-saving corporate messiah. You must present yourself as a professional colleague, and you will have about 30 minutes to be convincing in that role. Therefore, in addition to being relaxed and confident and avoiding bad speech habits, remember the following:

- Keep your hands in your lap. Using gestures to illustrate the points you are making is distracting in the extreme.

  Try it sometime when talking with a friend: Wave your hands around like a mime. Then notice how the person you're speaking to watches your hands, not your eyes. Surely your message will not be heard as clearly. The calculated use of gestures is effective when you're speaking before a large audience. Many in the audience won't be able to see how your facial expressions change to reinforce your message, but they'll notice the emphasis your hand movements provide. But this just doesn't work during an interview.

- Maintain eye contact. Staring off into space while you answer questions might be appropriate if a response in the form of a long, thoughtful discourse is called for. It rarely is. Simple, direct answers to questions are all that's needed. If you are an experienced salesperson, you'll want to keep eye contact so you can observe how your pitch is being received. (You'll also want to observe the interviewers' body language.)

- Don't overdo it. A certain amount of self-promotion in your presentation is expected. No one wants to work with a person who does not take considerable pride in his or her accomplishments. And, it's understood that you're trying hard in the time allotted you to get across how very much you know. But this can easily lead to long, rambling answers that create uncertainty as to how much you really do know.

The rule is, keep your answers short. Yes or no to every question asked you, followed by, at most, one or two sentences of explanation. If you really know your stuff, this will present no problems, and if elaboration is needed, most interviewers will ask for it. In other words: *when you're asked what time it is, don't explain how the clock works.*

If you aren't completely sure what the question is, ask for clarification—once, then give your best answer. Ask for clarification twice, and you'll be considered dim. Also, in addition to yes and no answers, you're entitled to a couple of I Don't Know answers per interview. Everyone hates to give that answer, for fear of revealing a lack of knowledge in a critical area. But deficiencies in knowledge can be overcome. A tendency to fabricate can create more serious problems, and this can be particularly dangerous in our modern techno-world. If, for example, you're asked about your familiarity with a particular technique, state precisely the extent of your knowledge and experience. If you exaggerate at all, you may be taken at your word and be given more responsibility than you can handle after you've been hired.

Leave if the interview gets really rough. Occasionally you'll encounter interviewers who make up their minds about applicants in the first few minutes of your time together, then use the rest of the interview as a torture session. The questions will become rude and often personal, seemingly with no correct answers being possible. It's possible that the interviewer may be putting you under stress to see how gracefully you respond. And, it's also possible that you'll thrive under such pressure, giving as good as you get and emerging—if you survive—with a job offer. That's the exception rather than the rule, however. Most often, the interviewer has decided, possibly before the interview began, that he doesn't want to have anything to do with you; he's doing the interview as an accommodation to his boss or to someone in Human Resources who does like you. In other words, you're dead before you begin, and once you have figured this out, there is absolutely no point in continuing. Make a dignified quick exit, with your self-respect intact.

After you've gotten past the first two interviews, you may be sent around to talk with some of the other professionals who could be your future colleagues. As they listen to you and watch you, these people will be asking themselves these questions:

- We are having a late dinner with clients in Los Angeles after an afternoon flight out from New York, on a day that began with a 7:00 A.M. staff meeting. We are all dead tired, but we have to strike just the right balance of conviviality and professionalism. Can this guy do that for us?

- The next day, we have to make our formal presentation to the client. The rest of us are too worn out to talk above a whisper. He has to do most of the talking and answer questions for an hour. He has to come across as relaxed, confident, and utterly competent. Can he?

- We have four more similar meetings in three days. In between the meetings, our team will be together, talking shop, preparing for the next meeting, unwinding after we're done. At the end of the week, will this person be a member of the team or will he still be an outsider?

Finally: Everything about this person seems great: solidly professional, polished interpersonal skills. But—can he PRO-DUCE for us? Does he have that extra element of obsession that sets someone who is driven to lead and succeed apart from a follower in the pack? The person who can show that extra, entrepreneurial spark will win out every time over the one who impresses as competent and collegial but not driven, not a standout.

The Career Track

You hope you'll get to the point where you'll have multiple job offers. If it works out that way for you, one of the most important considerations in comparing the offers is each job's career path. It's important to know what you can expect in each job, because in many companies there are fewer opportunities for advancement than ever before. This is one more result of the streamlining of business operations in the 1990s, as multiple layers of management are compressed into fewer and fewer steps on the ladder of success.

So you have to inquire what's in store for you if you succeed as spectacularly as you know you're going to, in the job you know you're about to be offered. When can a promotion reasonably be expected—at the very least, what's the range of time in years? Is it two to three years or one to five years or is it more vague than that? What does it take in terms of performance? Are outstanding performance reviews all that's required, or are there also specific types of assignments you'll have to take on and master? What career paths were taken by those to whom you'd be reporting?

There is a real possibility that instead of a promotion, your first reward for outstanding performance might be a lateral transfer. This wouldn't necessarily be bad, if it is part of a progression that could lead to a major promotion. But ask if that's the way things work at that company. Ask, too, if there's any specific training or education that you now lack that could taint your upward mobility. This may not be a formal requirement, but you may hear something like this, which amounts to a formal requirement: "Well, in the last 15 years, no one's moved up to that slot who didn't have a law degree." So, at least, you've been warned.

By now you should have enough information to know what

it's going to take to rise in the company, whether it's a huge multinational corporation or a much smaller operation. There is one other important question to ask your interviewers: Is regular relocation part of the normal career progression? If so, how often does it take place, and what choice is given in new assignments? If you get indications that you're going to be moving every three or four years for the next couple of decades, you'll have to think long and hard about how that could affect your lifestyle, particularly if you're married and have a family.

During your interviews, be sure to casually but carefully check out the information you're being given by others about the career path. A headhunter may be able to clue you in on a company's reputation for keeping the commitments it makes to advance outstanding professionals, or you may know people who work there now in other departments. Are they optimistic or pessimistic about their futures? If they're not hopeful, is it because they're mediocre performers or because they genuinely feel trapped in place?

In smaller, family-run companies, the feeling of being trapped can arise because family members occupy key, senior positions. This may not bother you if those positions are far above anything you aspire to, but if a company has a reputation for promoting family members regardless of their competence, the future of the company could be uncertain at best.

In the final analysis, the career path is a very important element of a job, and a careful assessment of all the elements that matter most to you will tell you how well you are likely to fit into any new situation. We'll return to the formal process of job assessment in Chapter Nine.

How to Tell When You're Getting Close

During the course of many interviews, you may wonder if there's a way to find out if you're scoring with the sales pitch you're making, and you're getting close to receiving an offer. Offers are rarely made on first interviews, so you shouldn't expect any indications during your screening interview, or in your first interview with people whom you'd be working for. You can expect an answer, however, to one reasonable question: When will a decision be made? If that time passes and you've heard nothing, an inquiry should tell you whether a decision has been delayed, or if you're out of the running.

The best indication that you're progressing toward an offer comes when you're brought back for second or even third interviews. If the discussions turn to specific terms and conditions of employment, but a formal offer still hasn't been hinted at, then it may be time to try what salespeople call a "trial close." This means that when terms and conditions are mentioned by the interviewer, you should say something like, "I always thought it was best to defer discussion of those matters until an offer was on the table. Are we close to that point now?" Or, "If we can resolve these points, are you prepared to make an offer?"

If you have misread the situation, if the intention was just to give you additional information, you may be greeted by a cool silence. If that happens you can simply back off and move on to another subject. But if the feedback is at all positive, you have your answer: You're getting close; real close.

Handling Age Discrimination

If you're over 40, certainly if you're over 50, somewhere during the interview process, obliquely or directly, you will probably encounter age discrimination. It is a fact of life in American business, and it's as easy to spot as it is difficult to do anything about.

You will hear it expressed often in the course of job hunting, and usually in terms like these: "Oh, Mr. Smith, we really are impressed with your background, but, frankly, you have too much experience for what the position requires." And, "Wow, Ms. Jones, you have a terrific résumé, and if anything, you're overqualified."

What cruel, patronizing, and inane comments those are! You've been job hunting for weeks, maybe months, and you know you can do the job and it interests you and you need the work, and you don't regard it as a temporary job. But management may not see it that way; they may rationalize turning you down on the grounds that you'll be gone as soon as "something better" comes along. Maybe, maybe not. But what if that "something better" is within the company? Isn't that a win-win situation for everybody? And in this intensely competitive new world economy, how is it possible for any company to have too many people who have "too much experience"?

But, fine, it's there, it's been expressed. There are at least three ways to handle it. First, you can give in, walk away without pushing through to a job offer. Or, you can try a little hardball, by responding, "Look, I'm sorry, I disagree, it sounds like you have a problem with my age. Is that what you're saying?" Then make similar remarks to the superior of the interviewer making the comment. Third, you can attempt to finesse the issue, to your advantage, in this manner: "I'm glad we agree I'm fully qualified. In this day and age, I don't think there is such a thing as 'overqualified,' do you? What I'm fully qualified to do is produce for you at top speed from my first day on the job, and for the long term." Make sure that message gets conveyed up the line, and push hard to be considered further. Not infrequently, there will be more overt indications, as in, "When did you say you graduated from college?" Or even, blatantly, "How old were you on your last birthday?"

There's no point lying about your age. It is a lie too easily found out. But neither is there any reason not to challenge their questions. To the inquiry about your date of birth, you say, firmly, "Whoa! You know you shouldn't be asking questions like that. Now, do we proceed, or do I just send a letter about this conversation to the Equal Employment Opportunity Commission?" If everything's gone well until that point and goes rapidly downhill thereafter, make a written complaint to the company's head of personnel—*not* to the interviewer's immediate supervisor.

It makes sense to push these objections as far as you can; you'll feel better for having done so. However, it usually doesn't pay to go farther every time you think you've been turned down because of your age. You will find discrimination very hard to prove, time consuming, expensive, and above all, distracting.

What you can do is avoid looking and acting like an old fuddy-duddy. I know people in their early sixties who are still getting promoted, who still bring a youthful zest to their jobs every day. And I've worked with people in their thirties with the attitudes of a 90-year-old and the energy level of a snail.

If you have gotten out of shape as you've aged, you now have a problem. If you are not seriously into some kind of regular, rigorous aerobic exercise, you're going to have difficulties, because it's going to be ever harder for you to sustain the levels of energy and enthusiasm that you'll need to stay competitive. You need to look trim and energized. Because the pace of job searching is naturally not as hectic as everyday business life, it's easy to put on weight after you've been fired. Check the poundage every other day. Reduce intake, immediately. Step up your exercise, immediately.

What if you're bald? Should you get a toupee? The answer is, whatever feels most natural for you, whatever looks best on you and makes you feel most comfortable. Color your hair? Again, if you want to, by all means do. There are now plenty of easy-to-apply, natural-looking coloring products on the market.

If you have any other impediments, they should be corrected as soon as possible. Don't squint; get glasses (contacts only if they're completely comfortable). Don't try to read lips; *get a hearing aid.* There are many good reasons for a relatively young person to be hard of hearing; don't try to fake it.

Above all, don't talk old. When you're asked about a problem, there's no need to respond, "I had a similar problem when I was at GM in '47 . . ." What's the point, old-timer? The questioner's interested in what you think, not where you were when you first thought it! Impress with your experience; don't scare people off with how long ago you acquired it.

In the end, if you're persistent, a little hard-nosed, and willing to work at it, age discrimination is a barrier you can overcome. Just don't pretend it's disappeared in this "enlightened" age, and don't accept it for a minute.

Remember that no matter how well you prepare and how good at interviewing you become, you will be turned down more often than not. But a high batting average in interviewing is not important. One success is all it takes!

CHAPTER SEVEN

The Pros and Cons of Networking

A network of contacts is indispensable to your recovery and future security. You have one now, whether you know it or not. It is in that card index file of business contacts and telephone numbers that you should have thrown into your briefcase the minute you knew you were being terminated.

Now it is passive—names and numbers. Your job is to activate it and to expand it, to turn it into a live, two-way instrument for the exchange of information about every element of career development. Your first priority is to use what you took away with you in your recovery, but paying attention to the long-term development of your network will pay off for you again and again.

Networking is much talked about by those in and around job markets. It is a means of establishing and maintaining communications with people who have information about decision makers, developments, trends and other relevant information, who can help you identify, track down, and secure jobs, and who you can similarly help.

Its most serious advocates and practitioners insist that networking must be a formal process, involving elaborate record keeping, written contact reports, multiple classifications of contacts, and tickler files to stimulate regular follow-up calls.

The objective of the networking process is to keep you current and fully informed of all significant changes in your segment of the job market. In that way, when the time comes to move, out of choice or necessity, you will know who to call, what to do, and what to say to move to a new position with a minimum of disruption to your career. In these uncertain times, that's an objective worth serious effort. I knew one human resources professional who claimed to spend 25 percent of his time doing networking. As important as it is for this specialist, it's easy to exaggerate its potential payoffs for you, and difficult to be certain that your network will work the way it's supposed to when you need it. If you make cautious, carefully thought-out commitments to networking, you will be more satisfied with the results, particularly if you recognize that it's one part of taking control of your career; it must be integrated with the other parts.

There are several aspects of networking you'll probably find useful; others, you'll probably conclude, are a waste of time. For instance, I once worked with two people who tried to identify by cold calling a certain number of potential new contacts every week. The number was not small—5 to 10 people, week in, week out. They were contacted by telephone or computer, and the message was simple and straightforward: "I'm networking; do you want to join mine? Can I join yours? Let's exchange résumés." Positive responses were often followed up by additional calls and sometimes by meetings.

These people, who I suspect are in the minority, are networking mavens. They always operate their networks at a high state of readiness, as though a job-market catastrophe was perpetually imminent. That can be tiring and counterproductive, and it's hard to maintain confidentiality when your lines are always open. A risk is that you could become just a general nuisance to those whose cooperation you want. Another is that networking can become such a distraction that your job performance suffers.

It's hard to consider networking that is this formal and open to be particularly useful for most employed people. But when you're unemployed, you must use whatever network you have. What is useful is an organized categorization of every business contact you make, no matter how you make it—over the phone, across a negotiating table, in a bar, or at a convention. If there is anything more than the most rudimentary personal and professional interest, it is a contact worth noting and following up on.

It's also important consciously and continually to expand your contacts in every way possible, within your company and on the outside. Seminars, trade associations, service clubs, political parties, and social clubs should all be considered in your plan. You should concentrate on whichever of these seem to interest you most and enable you to make the most productive use of your time.

Expanding your network with active memberships in professional and trade associations requires more than just your attendance at meetings once or twice a year. You also have to volunteer for committee work, run for office if asked, or take on tasks others may not want to do. This should be a "win-win" situation for you. It should help you do better in your current job and augment your network.

Following up with contacts is something those who are really serious about networking do quite aggressively: résumés, references, the whole bit. Again, that's overkill most of the time. Instead, scrutinize each new contact by asking this question: Based on what I've learned, if I needed a new job tomorrow, could this person get me an interview? Rate your response, from "5," "Could hire me on the spot," to "1," "Couldn't get me a towel from the ladies room."

Regardless of the rating, if you're at all interested in the individual as a professional, stay in touch. A follow-up note after your initial meeting and a "how're-you-doing-here's-what-I've-been-doing" letter once a year will do nicely. Reassess the ratings in your file every year; peoples' status does change. After a card has been rated "1" three years running, toss it.

For higher ratings, a different kind of follow-up is called for. Although you must be careful not to appear too pushy, it's fine to express a greater interest by writing more about yourself and your accomplishments and interests, and more than once during the year. As long as these don't turn into monthly missives, you're not likely to wear out your welcome. Nor will you be unwelcome if, once or twice a year, you take your high-rated contacts to lunch. This must, however, be a two-way street. You must from the beginning express real interest in learning about what they are doing, in learning from them, and in learning how you can help them.

Don't be surprised, however, if at the end of the year, in appraising your contacts' ratings, you find you have many more "1"s than "4"s or "5"s. At least if you make your appraisals realistically, you'll find that's the case. That's simply because most people won't be in a position to help you to relocate, or will show no serious interest in doing so. All the more reason therefore, for prudently, professionally expanding your network. The number of "5"s will remain relatively low but in absolute terms will expand, and these will be your real nuggets, to be cherished and cultivated.

The names in your business contacts file are your first line of defense, but not the only one. No acquaintance should be off-limits as a potential source of information about new jobs (except, perhaps, a hostile ex-spouse). Family, neighbors, fellow parishioners, any person with whom you are friendly enough to exchange information on subjects more serious than tomorrow's weather; these can be useful sources of leads. Not high-percentage sources, to be sure, and you may have to give them more background on the kinds of contacts you need than you would to a professional associate. But if you're patient, not too pushy, and are willing to work with them, they too can help uncover useful contacts.

There's another important point about networking that's as obvious as it is ignored. The best way to get yourself networked is to become that figure of fable, Outstanding Person In Your Field. If you become recognized by your peers and superiors in your company and industry, you will be plugged into networks whether you know it or not. You will be added to many "short lists" of people to be contacted when vacancies arise or new positions are created. This may not always help at the critical times when you need it most, but it is certainly better than having your name evoke blank stares when the "Who should we consider?" question comes up.

When and how do you activate your network? There are some who maintain that their networks are always ready to go to work for them to generate instant, genuine job leads. That level of readiness is too much for most people to sustain, if it can be sustained at all. You cannot constantly be on the alert for the next professional calamity, but it does pay to be alert for warning signals (several of these were discussed in Chapter One), but having a hair trigger in these situations can do more harm than good. You will quickly deplete your stock of network contacts if you always go popping off at the first sign of bad news. Calm, rational judgment is called for at all times. Of course, you don't want to be caught off guard, but there's no 100 percent effective protection against a surprise assault on your career.

After recognizing one or more of the warning signals discussed in Chapter One, and becoming convinced that they are serious, you should start transmitting out along the network, without panic but with purpose. If you haven't been fired, make that clear: "They continue to do well by me, but I have simply gone as far in this job and this company as I think I can." And if you have been let go, don't try to hide it: "Sure, I was part of that cutback," or, "My boss just felt a change was necessary." Don't hide it, but don't blow it out of proportion, either. Your unemotional conveying of this information will also send this message: "Hey, it's not ideal, but it happens. Can we move on?"

Going on Red Alert

There are times when the initiative will be in others' hands. Then you will have to use your network in a different way. I'm not referring to those instances, discussed previously, when you must make the network work for you. I'm talking about seemingly innocuous events that may make you want to move, fast.

What should put you on Red Alert are certain personnel changes, which could result in sudden changes in your status. Let's consider the implications of two of them:

- A new immediate supervisor

- A new CEO

You've had a solid working relationship with your boss for several years. Not perfect, but pleasantly productive. Then one day he's gone, and his replacement is a colleague who formerly worked on your level. You haven't had a particularly close relationship with the new person, but there hasn't been, from your perspective, any animosity, either. You're certain you will be able to work together.

Except that's not how the new manager sees it. A day, a week, or a month after this person takes over, you find yourself on the receiving end of this: "Look, Jim, I know that you and I have worked here for some time, and we've gotten along well, but that's not the point. One of the reasons for my promotion is that I see the manager's job quite differently than my predecessor. And, Jim, I have to tell you plainly, I have no problem with your work, with what you've done, but I'm going to take this department in a different direction, and, Jim, I just don't see a future for you here."

There are two rational explanations for this action. First,

this person genuinely believes what she just told you, that what she could live with when you were just a coworker is intolerable when thinking about you as a subordinate. Second, it may be nothing more than the action of a newly elevated regent swiftly eliminating potential rivals for the throne. Either way, it doesn't help you.

The installation of a new CEO may not cause you to lose any sleep. Even at the level you inhabit now, you probably consider yourself too lowly to be deserving of any particular attention. It's just that the new CEO's priorities may have a direct impact on you, regardless of how invisible you may think you are. I am not suggesting you go on Red Alert when the new CEO is from inside your company and assumes office as part of a normal management succession. The time to snap to attention is when the new chief is an outsider. It is the clearest indication you need of the board of directors' dissatisfaction with the way the company has been run.

You have to find out from any sources available what exactly the new CEO did in his or her last job. Did they reduce staff? If so, how quickly? By what means—the offer of voluntary retirement packages for older employees, by attrition, or by outright terminations? Or did they simply reorganize the function your department performs out of existence?

It is often a new CEO's first priority to reduce "head count"—nice phrase—across the board, and swiftly. It is amazing how fast a determined executive can move. I'm aware of one situation where the new CEO of a major company had an initial reduction of 5 percent decided on and all names identified within 30 days of his arrival.

In a less immediately threatening level, what's the new CEO like as a person? Are they one of those people who's in the office by 6:30 A.M. every morning, and wants to be able to reach out to anybody before 7:00, while you're one who must jump-start their heart to get into motion before 9:00 A.M.? You may be in for a rough ride. Or are they one of those intense executives who believes that every encounter with a subordinate should be a high-stress interview, roughly equivalent to the interrogations that were given by the KGB? You may then want to get out before your stomach becomes a high-production ulcer farm.

Or, you might not. That's right, you may not want to take any action at all. Your new boss, even if a former associate, may turn out to be the best professional friend you've ever had. The new CEO may make moves that will make upward moves for you more likely.

The point is, going on Red Alert means getting ready to move swiftly on the basis of solid evidence that you may be hit or may not want to stay. While you're deciding, you may want to quietly tune up your network to get current on jobs available that would be a good fit for you, that you might move into quickly. You may not want to start interviewing at this time, but you may want to talk with people who can get you hiring interviews.

You want to be in the same position as those Strategic Air Command bombers that used to be on runway alert. They weren't going to wait until enemy missile warheads arrived overhead before they took off; they were going to start rolling as soon as they saw clear indications that the rockets had been launched.

That's exactly how you should position yourself. You would rather not have to start rolling toward a new job. But you must know what to look for on your personal radar screen, know how to interpret what shows up there, and know when to avoid false starts. Nothing will wear out your network faster than using it when it's not absolutely essential. Nor will anything make you look more astute than seeing a change coming and acting in anticipation of it, rather than reacting.

To the extent that your network produces positive results for you, it may be because you were always aware that networking is a two-way street. You allowed yourself to be networked, and you helped others get a leg up in the process. That's nothing more than the Golden Rule in action.

A Network of Excellence

Are you interested in a form of networking that probably won't help your recovery, may never provide any tangible benefits, yet could result in developing business contacts that are deeply satisfying solely for professional reasons. If so, consider a Network of Excellence. This network glows from the conscious cultivation of the best people in your field, at your level and just above it, in your company and in others.

The objective is to become familiar with the work of those who are the best at what you do. You'll communicate with them by whatever means seem appropriate at the time. It may be after a speech at a convention, a call after the individual's work is mentioned in the news, or a complimentary letter about an article in a professional journal. Your level of attention will never be intense enough to be intrusive, just high enough to be flattering in a professional way.

Your work will have to be good enough to warrant the other person's returning your attention; otherwise you will not only be wasting your time, you may by your own efforts acquire a reputation as an amateur. But if you are professional enough, you may be rewarded with some of the most stimulating exchanges you'll ever experience. This network will help sustain your enthusiasm and keep you abreast of the most advanced thinking in your field.

In all your contacts, never mention anything about any job. If you are asked about your job, anything about it other than the purely professional aspects, respond as briefly as you can, with utmost modesty. Never take the initiative. You have established this network to fuel your professional growth. That is all.

Networking has an important place in everyone's plans to take control of their careers. It is most useful to you when you use it to act rather than react; and if you spend as much time actively helping others, you're playing the game as it was meant to be played.

CHAPTER EIGHT

When You've Been Out a Year

A close associate once had to make a difficult decision. He had lost his job and after two months in outplacement was just beginning to generate interviews. Then, in the space of 10 days he had two excellent interviews, both of which he felt would eventually lead to job offers.

One soon did. It was a solid position in a company with an excellent reputation for treating its employees well. There were two drawbacks. First, he would have to take a 10 percent pay cut. Second, he would have to spend up to two hours commuting each day, each way. The pay cut he felt he could live with, but the idea of driving four hours every day was mind-boggling.

The second job was less than an hour from his home and a substantial salary increase was involved, and he wanted it. He had to find out more about what his chances were, so he talked to the staff person who had conducted the screening interview and was told, "You meet all the requirements for the job as they are written in the specifications, or we wouldn't have invited you in. You are what your résumé says you are. Beyond that I cannot go, except to say this: There will be several other candidates. In about 30 days, when I've seen them all, I'll meet with my boss to discuss their qualifications—yours included. She'll decide who the finalists will be."

My associate did not want to take any new position on an interim basis, because he felt that this would be unprofessional in every respect. So the decision was a difficult one. In the end, he chose the "bird-in-the-hand" option. His reasoning was as follows: "I like the second job, and I'd do well in it. I'm qualified for it, they agree. But that's all. I have no other advantages. I have no one on the inside who knows me and can speak up for me. There's no way I can 'wire' the job. I know nothing about the interests or requirements of the woman who'll be deciding who to hire, and I've concluded that there's no way I can find out. So I can't be any more responsive than I've been. At best I have a 50-50 chance of getting the job. That's not good enough."

In the event, his judgment proved prescient. Months later he learned that he would not have been included among the finalists. The screener was quite candid: "You were well qualified and you made a good impression, and we'd like to stay in touch. There may be something else we can do together another time. But the position you were applying for—it was just your luck that there turned out to be other applicants who were exceptionally well qualified. One had more qualifications than we felt we'd be able to get for what we had to offer. That one we hired."

My associate had been tempted to wait, but he is now glad he didn't. He has been commuting for two years, but sees a good chance he'll be able to find an acceptable position closer to home within the next 12 months. He has even used his drive time productively, thanks to two instruments he uses effectively as business tools: a cellular telephone and a cassette player. And, *he has kept the cash flow coming*.

The question is, did he have other options that he ignored, or gave up on too soon? He may have, and we'll discuss them shortly. But you won't be able to convince this person that he made the wrong choice. He is working. He has a financial plan, and the two-month hiatus did minimal damage to it. He's making regular investments with certain objectives in mind. It's now going to take him longer to reach his objectives, but he's staying with the plan. Twelve, not 10 years from now, he figures his investment income will be sufficient to provide about 50 percent of his income, and that will give him the cushion he needs to try some other things he's long dreamed of, such as consulting, teaching, and writing. He didn't want to jeopardize those dreams by continuing a long and possibly fruitless search for the "ideal" job.

Of course, this man acted as though those two jobs were the only prospects on the horizon. If that was true, wasn't his horizon set unrealistically close? If he was working at his recovery the way we've agreed he should have been, isn't it likely that in two more months, or two more months beyond that, he would have, should have generated other, better job offers?

There is no one right answer, one that makes sense for anyone, regardless of their situation. I strongly believe in the advice I offered earlier: reemployment within 60 days should be your highest priority. The reasons for that advice have been validated by experience.

It is too easy to become an unsalable commodity in the job market. Job hunting requires a major effort and a high level of enthusiasm to be sustained effectively. After your intense efforts have produced interviews but not job offers, which is to be expected, it's easy to get discouraged and slack off. The frequent result is that fewer contacts are made and less enthusiasm is conveyed in the selling of yourself. You may sound less like someone who is convinced beyond a doubt that they're the best person for the job, and more like someone who's asking for a favor.

For many, however, such advice is irrelevant, because there is no way everyone is going to become reemployed within two months. There is no way to determine when a person will complete the most important part of his or her recovery and get back to work. What's most important is to begin with a recovery/rehiring plan that sets what you think are reasonable time limits on all the key elements: résumé writing, mailing; personal contacts, follow-up contacts; lead generation; first, second interviews; and receiving and evaluating job offers.

The time limits, however loosely they are set, are checkpoints at which you should stop and assess your progress, particularly when you've moved beyond the points you can control. The magic threshold, the point at which you cross over into some sort of netherworld, seems to be a year. Some think that if they haven't found work by the end of their first year out, they aren't going to. Then they start to thrash about and perhaps even drop out of the job market, and their purposeful, focused job search seems to grind to a halt.

This is what they think people are thinking about them: "Wow! It's been a year since you left your last job? What do you do, sell air-conditioners to Eskimos?" But the proper reaction on passing this milestone is, SO WHAT, if you are proceeding according to your plan. Remember, I advised making your Transition Budget's time horizon a year.

But what is your objective? When do you expect to be back at work? Another six months? Another year? There is still no answer that's right for everyone. There may be nothing wrong with your recovery plan. You may be fully satisfied with the way it's unfolding. It's just that sometime around the first anniversary of your termination, if not sooner, you should take enough time off from your job search to reassess the plan—every element of it.

Before beginning that review, it's a good idea to step back and assess something that's not a formal part of the plan but is important to its success: your psychological status. How are you coping? Is your enthusiasm waning? It's natural that it would, but you must renew your efforts to sustain it, you know that. Being down on yourself can have a negative impact on everything you're working on, from the number of résumés you send out to the way you follow up on them. Then your chances of getting a job will be decreasing, not increasing.

There are many ways you can get yourself psyched up again; if you perceive this as a problem, focus on it now, by taking a complete break from your efforts and engaging in any activity that will refresh you while it takes your mind off what you've been doing. Your slippage may have been so gradual that it went unnoticed. Provide yourself with a means to check this by putting a few precise benchmarks in the plan: number of calls made to "5" category contacts per week; number of new leads developed; number of résumés sent out. Keep track of your progress against the benchmarks. It's busywork but not wasted work.

Beyond any faltering in the effort, there seem to be a number of reasons for long-term unemployment.

- Failure to organize an intelligent, coherent recovery effort. This is not from lack of interest in continuing on in their professional field—they have no desire to go back to what they were doing a decade ago—but from lack of knowledge. They're very willing to work hard at getting back to work, but they don't know where to begin. They haven't been provided with outplacement counseling and, although they've made inquiries, few friends have been able to help.

- Believe it or not, a major problem is an unwillingness to ask for help. For reasons beyond my comprehension, some people are too shocked, shy, or afraid of rejection to ask for help. They wait for the telephone to ring. Their job search is limited to responding to newspaper ads. They can't admit to others that they're out of work, so they can't begin to take the initiative and go out actively into the market.

- Some people simply aren't aggressive about conducting a job search. Even though they were white-collar workers, they return "temporarily" to a trade they may have left years before, because they are disillusioned—by what happened to them, by people they think they'd have to come in contact with again, or by the "rat race." So while they have mounted some kind of recovery effort, it is not their number-one priority. Even if they've taken a cut of 30 percent or more and gone into a dead-end job, they seem content. They react as though shell-shocked.

- Some people have asked for too much. They've conducted an effective search, and been on many interviews. But every time they've come close to receiving an offer, they have sent clear signals that they weren't willing to compromise on negotiating positions the other party considered unacceptable. This is a potentially serious problem, because the word may have spread: This person really has an inflated opinion of himself.

- Personal offense. Something that turns people off quickly. This problem could be anything from a severe case of body odor to talking too quickly or mumbling. If you sense you have such a problem, try to find out exactly what it is. Then, even if it will take time to effect a cure, make the effort. You're out of luck if you don't.

- People whose occupations vanished, or at least became in great oversupply. I've seen this happen to government workers who specialized in one program for many years. When the program was cut, they had few transferrable skills, and were a long time finding other work.

Assuming none of the preceding is your most serious problem, reconsider every decision you've made in the last 12 months: You turned down an offer that required relocation? You declined a position that would have required your doing something different, with lower status and less pay? Are you willing to change any of those decisions now? If you are, will the change now increase your chances of finding a job quickly? This last question deserves special consideration, because it will tell you whether or not you've painted yourself into a corner. If your particular working universe is small enough or specialized enough, that is a real risk. You could have become unemployable on your terms. Then the question for you is as simple as it is blunt: What changes must I make?

If you're still reluctant to reverse earlier decisions, by all means seek second opinions about your failures. Recontact some of the people you spoke with three or six months ago. Did you have screening interviews that never led to anything else? If you don't know why, it's worth some telephone time to try to find out; call the people with whom you spoke. You have nothing to lose.

What about the friends and business contacts you asked for advice and guidance? Did you follow their advice? What suggestions do they have to offer now? Do not be embarrassed to call them again. There's nothing wrong with admitting a temporary failure, but there's a lot wrong with accepting it.

While you continue your search, and however you redirect it, you should now consider part-time employment—whether or not your financial condition makes this an imperative. This means steady work you can do for 15 to 20 hours a week, at times other than the usual 9:00 A.M. to 5:00 P.M. business hours. Since you are continuing on diligently with your job search, this will make for long, tiring weeks. For that reason alone, some advise against part-time work unless it's absolutely essential. You will, they argue, be too tired to make a professional appearance during the day, and the quality of your job search will suffer at a time when it needs to be improved.

That may or may not be true, but even if it is, after a year you may get a real psychological boost from "permanent" part-time employment. Even if the work is not comparable to your last job, you will have proved again that you are worth something to somebody. Don't downplay the improvement this can bring to your outlook. The end result could be a job search that's approached with renewed enthusiasm, even if the hours devoted to it are reduced, because there's less of an element of desperation in your search.

As long as you have a plan for getting a job, are monitoring its implementation regularly, and are conscious of the consequences of the decisions you're making, no one can criticize you for not accepting the next job offer that comes along. And in case you've been thinking of taking that job, let's think about why that could be the worst decision you could make— despite my back-to-work-in-60 days advice.

Is accepting a considerable downgrade in a full-time position a tolerable alternative to the prospect of long-term unemployment? There are serious drawbacks to taking a job for which you are plainly overqualified. The major concern is that you'll drop so far down the career ladder that you will not recover in your working life, financially or professionally, even if you rationalize the fall as a "different job" or a "lateral transfer."

A related risk is that, even if you're hired into such a position by a willing management, you could find that you are substantially older than your peers. If you aren't able to bridge this generation gap and fit in easily with the new group, you may find yourself isolated, and unable to develop the close working relationships that are so essential to career growth.

Finally, you may become impatient and frustrated as you confront daily tasks that you consider menial. This frustration, if it surfaces, will be destructive; you'll appear impatient and arrogant. Your superiors will eventually conclude they made a big mistake.

If this type of a situation is the most likely option still available to you, continued unemployment may be the lesser risk, if you can still suffer the financial consequences and if the businesses you are prospecting in are still growing and there are regular openings in your specialty. This is also true if your age isn't considered a handicap and if you are still generating productive leads and interviews.

The one-year unemployment benchmark is the point at which you should begin to make major reductions in your outlays, including selling your house and moving to a place that doesn't cost as much. These admittedly are not the best of times to be selling a house, at least not in most parts of the country. If a sale will result in the loss of your equity, work on other areas of expense reduction, while working with the holder of your mortgage on ways to reduce the burden of the payments temporarily—without selling.

A smaller mortgage at a lower rate can, however, produce noticeable savings. Compare these numbers: a $150,000, 30-year mortgage at 10.75 percent, and a $110,000, 30-year mortgage at 9.00 percent. The monthly payment on the first mortgage, excluding property taxes, is $1,400. On the $110,000 loan, the payment is $885; a $515 monthly reduction in outlays. This calculation doesn't take into account borrowing costs or other costs such as moving expenses, nor does it include the tax "benefits" of the larger mortgage. But the benefits to you, net, are still substantial. They will give you much more flexibility in holding out until the job you want comes along sometime in the future—if you think that future might be a distant one.

Finally—please do not get discouraged. No matter how much bad luck you've had until now, or how many choices you now believe you'd make differently, you have to believe that what's ahead is better than what you left behind.

That is what kept another friend going 15 years ago. He worked in a highly specialized profession and received top-notch marks for his work. But a nasty corporate reorganization left him out in the cold and determined to find another profession. He didn't have any idea about what that might be, or where to start looking—this was before outplacement services were widely available. In the months that followed he received several offers in his old specialty, which he turned down. Otherwise he was completely flexible; location, money, responsibilities, all were negotiable.

After 15 months, one of his "shot-in-the-dark" résumés produced an inquiry from an agency with words that were music to his ears: "What you do have, we're extremely interested in; what you don't have our client thinks you can be trained for. Have you ever thought about . . . ?" He hadn't, he did, there was a fit, an offer, and a new career.

CHAPTER NINE

Across the Finish Line

After sending out hundreds of letters, dozens of résumés, and surviving 15 or 20 screening interviews and half that number of follow-up interviews, you have received an offer. That is, the phone call or the letter says, if terms can be agreed on.

Of course you are thrilled. Perhaps not exhilarated—you were working toward multiple job offers—but satisfied that all your hard work is on the verge of paying off. Success is so close you can taste the champagne that you will soon be savoring at your victory dinner.

You are not home free yet, however. There are still tricky negotiations ahead, as each party jockeys for maximum advantage, each with issues that can be negotiated and issues that will be off-limits.

Do you have your list of issues? Have you decided where you're prepared to compromise and where you'll dig in your heels? Do you think you know what's on the company's list? Have you tried to find out?

Let's begin with your compilation. Exactly what goes on it is what is important to you; no one can write it for you. I can, however, suggest how to develop it. Write down every important part of your last job, from salary to each fringe benefit to your title. Wherever possible, quantify them: last salary—

target salary—"Will Accept" salary; and on down the list. Your list should have three headings:

LAST   TARGET   ACCEPTABLE

Leave space around each item on the "Last" list for your comments: "Great; sorry I had to lose that"; "Must be improved." If for any item your "Target" and "Acceptable" goals are identical—in other words you're telling yourself there's no room for compromise—ask yourself two questions: If I don't hit my Target, do I walk away? And, if I don't hit my Target with this item, is there any possible trade-off? In other words, is there anything I might ask for in another area in return for giving ground on this point?

You're now close to having a formal, rational approach to assessing the offer that will soon be before you. There are some additions to include on your list, additions that go beyond what is broadly defined as "the compensation package." Important things such as "growth potential" and "visibility," and more mundane matters like "support staff." Add those you consider important to your list, then rank them all as to *how* important they are, from "1," possible giveaway, to "5," nothing's more important.

Finally—in order to keep this from getting too complicated—put down what you know about where the company stands on each item on your list, or your impression of its stance. For instance, on vacation time: "Stated policy is three weeks first three years, four weeks beginning in year four. Husband has four weeks now; will see if they can get me four weeks sooner." And, "support staff: First impressions aren't good; receptionist ignored me first five minutes I was there; secretaries all yakking, none working."

Remember, these are just impressions, and they could change completely after further assessment. But they are what you have to go on now and they are part of the picture you are developing.

Needed next is a formal written offer from the company, which covers all the points that are important to you. These points should be discussed before the letter is sent out, so that you don't have to go back and say, "Uh, gee, I forgot to mention _____ and it's kind of important to me . . . ?"

When the letter arrives, compare the points with the points on your list. Rank what's been offered using your Target columns as a guide, again using a 1 to 5 scale—1 being totally unsatisfactory and 5 being "great." If you have a bunch of 1's and 2's when you get to the bottom of the list, you have a problem; 3's and 4's make your decision easier, but shouldn't shut off further negotiations on any point you're still concerned about.

Assuming you've rated the offer point-by-point objectively (you'll only be hurting yourself if you fudge the ratings), should you even consider accepting an offer for a position that rates mainly 1's and 2's? Sure, it's conceivable, but why, then, did you go through the rating exercise? Those low numbers are sending you a message: YOU AREN'T GOING TO BE HAPPY IF YOU ACCEPT. Time then, to bow out politely, without burning any bridges: "Another time, perhaps; for now I think we're too far apart on too many important issues. Thanks for everything, etc." Although it's always possible that the company negotiator has been bluffing, the chances are this is where it ends. Back to work . . .

At some point in the hiring process, possibly before an offer has been made, or during earlier interviews, you may be asked what your current salary is. This can be a difficult and embarrassing question, particularly if you've been in a dead-end job with minimal increases for a few years.

Never give out this information. If you do, it may hurt your chances of getting a job, or getting the best possible salary. There are many ways of evading the question: "Well, I'm sure that if there's a good fit, the salary question will take care of itself." "I don't understand what my past history has to do with the requirements of this job." "Any numbers I could give you would be so difficult to compare that I just can't do it." "I'm more concerned with what I can bring to this new position." There are endless variations on these themes. Any graceful, polite evasion that gets the questioner to change the subject will suffice.

Unfortunately, some questioners will indicate (as some ads make clear) that if you don't answer, you will not be considered further. When confronted by that situation, you may want to end it right there: "Thanks, but no thanks." But, if for any reason you feel you have to respond, and your gut feeling is that you were earning well below the norm for the position, then an exaggeration is appropriate—and necessary.

There is a risk you'll be found out—your new boss could call your ex-boss (your ex-boss could also get into serious trouble for disclosing such information)—but it's the lesser risk. To be a little safe, you might add on a maximum of 15 percent to your old number. Then take a deep breath—and press on.

There's another piece of information you should never give out until an employer has made an offer: the names of your references. You may be asked to provide references early on in the selection process, by a headhunter or a human resources person at the company to which you've applied. There's no reason for the information references might provide until a decision has been made to offer you a job, so their names shouldn't be released until then.

It may be that there are a few people to whom you are very close, who know of your situation and have offered to help in any way possible. They may be used as references at any stage in the job-search process, even at the beginning when, for example, a headhunter has indicated that he cannot work further with you until you have provided references and they have been checked out. You must be certain, however, that these special references will not be turned off by repeated calls as your job search progresses.

Obviously, you should try to limit the frequency with which references are contacted. This means qualifying every potential situation when names are requested. If you're not impressed with the seriousness of the management recruiter, try to delay providing them. If they are requested at the beginning of the interview process with a potential employer, indicate that you would be pleased to provide good references at the time an offer is put on the table.

Preparing Your References

No matter how hard headhunters may try to pry the names of your references from you, limiting access to those names is very important to controlling your recovery. You may not get past first base with some headhunters unless they are able, early in the relationship, to talk with your references at length. In such cases, you have to assess what's likely to transpire after the references have been checked out. Is your personal profile just going into a data bank, or is the prospect of interviews clear on the horizon?

If a retainer headhunter has contacted you, and has indicated after a qualifying interview that she's considering you for the short list for an interesting position, by all means provide the names. But if you've initiated a contact with a contingency firm, and the firm's search is just beginning when the request is made, ask for a postponement: "I have the best references; you'll see that when the time comes. But it's possible our search may involve many interviews, and I'd like for my references not to be contacted until it's clear we're closer to job offers." That's as reasonable as you need to be. If you're pushed, pass: "Sorry, that's just not the way I work; thanks for your time. Bye-bye."

Controlling the contacting of references until they can make maximum impact for you is the objective of such exchanges with management recruiters. But timing is only part of maximizing their impact. Preparing them to be contacted is the other important part.

If you can meet with them face-to-face, do so. If that's not possible, a telephone conversation will do—at a time when neither of you is likely to be interrupted. The meeting has to be planned. Make sure that each reference receives a copy of your résumé several days before your meeting. It should be accompanied by an explanatory letter that covers a number of important points: the kind of job you're looking for; where you are in your search—just starting out, or already interviewing; when you think references might be contacted.

These points need to be repeated at the outset when you meet. You then have to move into the substance of your résumé: "I've tried to state my accomplishments as I see them. I'd be interested to know if there's anything about them you'd like to discuss further." What you're asking, of course, is if there's any claim in the résumé that's going to cause her to laugh hysterically when an important headhunter or someone from a company that's close to making you an offer reads it back to her.

You may think you know these people; that's why you're using them as references. Now you must find out how well you know them. If you don't, they could kill your chances of getting a job. So as your conversation moves along, try to steer it so that your references feed back your résumé to you in their own words. The more natural it sounds to you, the more it sounds like the genuine expression of respect of one professional for another, the safer you will be.

Tentative resistance to any claim or assertion you're making should cause you to immediately modify or delete it. Beyond that, anything other than broad and enthusiastic agreement should cause you to see red flags: Finish the conversation, then find another name for your list! That's why in-person meetings are much preferable. In addition to hearing what is said or not said, you can observe the body language, and you can provide feedback and see how it is received.

Although the support of your professional qualifications should be at the center of your conversation, you should not neglect the human side. Any competent reference checker will want to know, "What's this person *really* like?" It's important that you find out what your reference really thinks. They could think very highly of you professionally, and *think that's all that matters,* and so, when contacted and probed in this area, may respond offhandedly, "Oh, she's real serious; she really sticks to her work." Good-bye job offer! There goes the possibility of any further interest from a company that's looking for a gregarious team player who interacts easily with others. So explore more, until you're satisfied that anyone who calls your references will hear positive, supportive appraisals that will advance your chances of receiving a job offer. If you give in too easily on this point, you may find that your best sources of positive responses are being pestered for information in situations that probably aren't going to lead to job offers. Then you'll have to call them and say, "Thanks again; close, but no cigar." How many times do you think you can make such calls and not lose these people as references?

Assuming all these rocks and shoals are navigated safely, you are tiptoeing right up to the finish line. Be patient, be cool; don't assume that final negotiations have to be concluded quickly. Don't appear to be anxiously pushing for a quick resolution. You may desperately want to wrap things up in a couple of hours of negotiation, but it may work out better if you make your negotiating points, and don't press for an immediate response: "Look, you're offering X thousand a year. I'd really like to see 4 or 5 thou more, and that extra week's vacation is important to me, because that's how much my husband gets. We're a close family. Please let me know what you can do in these areas."

These are not the kind of issues that should be raised until the negotiations are well along, close to a climax, when both parties know that few major points remain to be settled. Your indicating that you do not require an immediate answer should tell the other party how important the issues are to you. And by all means, you should express once again your genuine interest in the position.

Their response may take a day, a weekend, or a week. If you haven't heard anything in a week, it's likely you may have turned them off. One way to reduce the chances of that happening is to keep the Human Resources screening interviewer apprised of the progress of negotiations, if you sense there might be difficulties. You are hoping, if your requirements have come to be considered excessive, that one of the people with whom you've interviewed will tip you off in time for you to back off. But never assume anyone inside the company can act as an intermediary in your negotiations.

If you have worked with a headhunter, however, you may have a useful go-between at your service. The higher up you are, the more active the headhunter's role is likely to be. Final negotiations for more senior positions will involve more complex and sensitive issues. Headhunters, with their knowledge of both parties, may at critical times help bring them together. If you are in the mid- to upper-five-figure range and working with a contingency recruiter, however, expect to be on your own.

So you've done all this work, have considered all the elements of the job that has been offered to you, realized some improvements, given concessions. Then, one day the phone rings and the voice on the other end says, "Mr. Dudgeon, I think we have a deal. If you can start in 10 days, we do have a deal."

Congratulations! You are back among the living! Now take that vacation that you put on the back burner when you started outplacement counseling. You've earned it, so enjoy it! Because when you return and start work, the real fun begins; the next phase of your recovery gets under way.

The most important part of your recovery is now behind you; you are working once again at a job that meets at least your minimum requirements. You can now wipe your brow and say to yourself, "Whew, I'm glad that's over." It is tempting to settle into that kind of relaxed attitude, but you will regret it if you do; recovery in the 1990s is an ongoing process. It did not end when you accepted the offer for the position you're now settling into, and it will not end when you choose your next position—2, 5, or 10 years in the future.

Recovering is oriented to the future as well as the present, because it must involve lifetime planning for your career. And since career planning has never been less predictable, continued activity on your part is required to protect yourself. The tense of the word *recovering* sums it up nicely: present conditional.

Consider just how satisfied you are with your brand new job. Don't lean back in your chair and say you're satisfied with any activity that brings in a paycheck. Do you plan to do anything about those category rankings on your list that only rated "1's" or "2's"? Or are you just going to ignore them, let them fester while they continue to unsettle you? Out beyond the first year, just how secure do you think the job will be, even assuming outstanding performance on your part?

Our controlling view is that you can never again feel as secure as you could have a generation ago; and thus you can't think of your recovery as a sprint race. You are indeed across the finish line, but only of the first heat—there are several more middle-distance runs to be finished.

In the remaining chapters, we'll discuss the important additional elements that are essential to your recovery. Then and only then can you begin to feel a little more secure.

CHAPTER TEN

Recovery: The Next Step

You've found a new job. You're satisfied with the compensation package, the work is manageable, your new colleagues seem amiable enough, and you see room to grow. And yet you know in your heart you do not want to abandon your job search. Here are a few reasons why you might feel that way.

- You might have lucked into a job in a declining industry and, although things might seem rosy in the near term, you're concerned about the future.

- Although the new position is in no way a demotion, it's not the real step up you genuinely feel you're qualified for, and want.

- You're convinced your professional specialty doesn't have a future, and even though you've been able to catch on again in that specialty quickly, you're also convinced the risks of staying in it are high.

These are all good reasons for not putting your job search in the deep freeze. You've probably acted prudently in latching on to something that is less than ideal but infinitely better than the prospect of long-term unemployment. But you won't really feel in control unless you take that next step.

The major benefit you will enjoy now is that you are looking while working. This situation has two advantages. The first, most obvious, is that you can be as choosy as you want to be. The second is that to a potential employer, you won't appear to be damaged goods.

But to that potential new employer you will indeed appear suspect if you try to move too quickly. It's recommended that for at least the first year to 18 months you focus on nothing but excelling in your new job. And unless the job is a high-visibility one in which you can quickly make a major track record, you may need to put other plans on hold for two years.

Even if you gain quick recognition as a world-beater in a year's time, understand that your renewed job search will have to be conducted differently. You should not even think about contacting key members of your network who helped land you your present job, to involve them in your renewed search. If they learn from other sources that you're making inquiries and ask you about them, respond casually: "I just want to be a bit more sensitive to what's going on in the marketplace than I have been. I never want to be caught flat-footed like I was before."

Recognize, too, that discretion is your number-one priority. Limit access to your résumé to those you trust completely. Be extremely careful who you talk to, and talk only in the vaguest generalities until you've qualified the individual, until you're sure there's a true mutual interest. In your present situation, names of references cannot be provided until you are certain that negotiations with your new company are close to completion.

If use of your existing network is precluded, who should you talk to? To new members of the network. Start adding them immediately. Try to help them now in any way you can; your turn will come many months from now. You can find them in places you must make special efforts to access: service clubs such as Rotary, Kiwanis, and Lions, and through volunteer work as well as professional societies and trade organizations. Once you have indicated you have time and are seriously interested, you'll have more offers to get involved than you can handle. That is the first step. The second step comes when you start asking your new acquaintances for direction and advice. You should begin these inquiries, most casually and discreetly, at a reasonable time after the acquaintances have been made, without making people feel you are using them.

If you have neglected your quest for excellence during this period, you will have made it more difficult for yourself in every way possible. If you can't look back at the end of each year with a feeling of pride at how much you've learned and accomplished, something's wrong.

Perhaps you're approaching the limits of the job. In any job, when your learning curve starts increasing at a decreasing rate, it's time to think about other things. You should be able to sense when you start to learn less, grow less, and enjoy it less. You cannot stop growing, ever. This concept may seem ridiculous to careerists, or dangerously bad advice to those who think of 15-year employees as "short-timers." But I know quite a few people who served more than a decade in their last jobs, and say now, "Never again. I don't know what I'll be doing five years from now, but it won't be this. When the time comes, I'll know and I'll decide where I go next."

A more difficult problem arises when you want to take the Two-Step to a different career. Then, in addition to everything else that's been discussed here, you have to take on an additional assignment. After deciding what you want to do next, go out and start doing it: part-time, evenings, Saturdays. For pay, for anyone in the area you've selected who's willing to take you on. For as long as it takes to get the experience needed to do it full time.

We're not talking here about second jobs taken strictly to supplement income, but about responsible positions that interest you, and through which you have a meaningful opportunity to acquire experience that can be transferred to a full-time job. You should have formed a clear idea of the career track you're switching to before you begin. You should be satisfied that the (part-time) job you're considering isn't a dead end, and can lead higher. This may take time, but if you stay with it, it shouldn't take long; and obviously, be prepared to bail out if you conclude that you have made a mistake.

Two-Step Risks: No Gypsies Need Apply

There is a risk to the Two-Step: you may be perceived as a corporate gypsy, an employee who always has his or her bags packed. To some potential employers, a résumé that shows frequent job changes for a person over age 30 is a real turnoff. Employers look for people who are interested in long-term relationships. Unfortunately, they may be deceiving you by implying they can commit to such a relationship. Twenty years ago, sure; 10 years ago, perhaps; today? Nonsense! If this issue ever arises during an interview, ask this question: "When was the last time you folks had staff cuts—any at all?" If the only response is awkward silence, you know that issue is off the table.

Another risk is that, no matter how satisfied you are, your job hunting could become a permanent distraction, and an unnecessary one. If you are really talented, it's been said, you'll never have to go looking for a job—the job will find you. Because of the intense competition for jobs today, that's less true than it ever has been. There are plenty of "really good" people out there, and they are at least likely to be invited to join the competition for any job openings. Excelling in whatever you do should be your first, second, and third priorities, but not your only priorities. If you do see something you want, you're going to have to go after it. Only then will you find out if others have a high opinion of you.

Getting Out While the Getting's Good

As you begin work again, it's important to consider what at the time may seem a silly question: Even if you are completely satisfied with the job you've just started and aren't interested in the "Two-Step," should you ever stop job hunting? Even after you have settled into a job you enjoy thoroughly and expect to be able to grow in for years to come, should all efforts to move up and move out be completely deactivated?

Without question, they should not be. Of course they should be geared down; your number-one priority is your new job. Now that your circumstances are better, you don't have to respond to newspaper ads. You do, however, have to respond to your network friends, to those who helped you get to this point. Do not wait for them to call you. Call them at regular intervals, ask how you can help. Keep those lines of communication open.

Be always alert for changes in your circumstances, changes that could affect your ability to control your career. If you are charging ahead professionally, you shouldn't worry too much as long as your performance is peak. But the happiest situation can change overnight, and if changes do occur, act, don't react. Reflect on this situation and you'll understand why. A few years ago a friend accepted the number-two position in a major department of a well-known nonprofit corporation. The number-one person was 61 years old, and made it clear that he was expected to retire at age 65. My friend, 20 years younger, accepted her job with two stipulations: the corporation did promote from within, and she was to be groomed by number one to move into his slot.

After she had been there just 10 months, however, another man was hired in the department who had experience identical to hers, except he had more of it. Nothing visibly changed. Her responsibilities were steadily growing, and number one was beginning to showcase her and delegate more to her. Yet within another 20 months my friend had left for a better job. Why? She didn't like the idea of surrendering control of her near-term future to someone else. She determined that, although her boss was still committed to her, the CEO had made no such commitment. The CEO, in fact, in the past had made it clear he wanted at least two candidates for every promotional opening—including, sometimes, outsiders.

Although she was confident of her ability to prevail in a competition with the newcomer—she estimated her chances of winning to be 60–40—she knew the decision could be made on the basis of factors other than her continued outstanding performance and her personality, which offended no one. So she left. Do you think she overreacted? Let's see. Her new job satisfied the growth criteria she'd set out—income and responsibility increases—but she was concerned that staying in this job would put the pace of her career growth at risk. Wanting to keep her career moving forward, she activated a quiet job search, not out of desperation but out of prudence, hedging the bet she'd made on her mentor.

This woman focused on the advantages of getting out now versus the need to get out later if she lost the competition and was passed over for number one. She could imagine reading the headhunters' minds: "This is the woman who was passed over after five years at the Fahnstock Foundation. I wonder what's wrong with her." What she couldn't assess clearly enough was the evolving situation at the Foundation, as it affected her, and that she was unwilling to accept. In comparable circumstances, neither should you.

My friend followed all the good rules of a highly discreet search by one who is ostensibly happily employed. She made direct contact with those in her network, closest to her, whom she hadn't used before. She identified leads from several sources and was able to develop them effectively. Those close contacts knew or were made aware of her professional progress. If they thought it at all curious that she was out looking again so soon, they had no reason to believe she was being pushed out the door. She made it clear that although she was ambitious, she was in no hurry to change. Her friends did consider her overly ambitious. The search might have taken longer, or because of the need to keep it quiet, might have failed completely. But in her case, she was able to establish herself as a valuable commodity in the market. When she left Fahnstock, she was able to make it appear as though she had been recruited, that she received an offer she couldn't refuse.

The moral: Everything can change. Turn the network down but don't turn it off—ever.

The Limits of Loyalty

In today's supercharged business environment, it doesn't take much to put your job at risk. In a downturn, many fewer companies are willing to hold professional staff levels constant in expectation of better days. Employees at companies that practice only temporary layoffs will consider themselves lucky. More likely than ever is the use of a recession—any kind of recession—to justify permanent reductions in "head count."

This isn't how it used to be. Although America has never had the tradition of "lifetime" employment common in Japanese enterprises, many types of jobs, particularly those in white-collar classifications, were considered much more immune to periodic downsizing than jobs on assembly lines. That has changed forever. While many assembly-line workers still have the protection of union contracts that offer some hope of an eventual return to work, most white-collar workers have absolutely no protection. Their jobs can be abolished permanently, in only a minute.

You may think you have a right to expect that loyalty will be a two-way street, but you are well on your way to the Land of Oz if you expect to see your loyalty consistently reciprocated more than a fraction of the time. You may have had a warm and mutually supporting relationship with everyone you ever worked for, and you may be as fortunate in the future. But if you should find yourself in a less fortuitous situation, you'll be able to adapt successfully if you define for yourself your limits of loyalty.

It's important to recognize that some kinds of loyalty are more important than others. You shouldn't expect a company today to be loyal to a mediocre employee with no desire to improve his or her performance, just because he or she has been with the company 20 years. Don't be too concerned if your company periodically fires or demotes its worst performers, as long as you're satisfied that the judging standards are reasonable (those who are at the bottom have been there for some time) and they've been given a reasonable time to improve. But if such prunings seem capricious and unrelated to performance, you should act accordingly. Unfortunately, even a healthy corporate culture that excludes such erratic behavior offers little long-term protection. That culture can change faster than you can say, "new CEO."

At a personal level, you shouldn't be too upset if your boss doesn't praise you to his peers whenever he has the opportunity to do so, even if your performance is always outstanding. It shouldn't upset you unduly if you aren't showcased as quickly as you think you should be, or if responsibility isn't heaped upon you as rapidly as you think appropriate. But you should set formal goals for your professional advancement— key benchmarks that are particularly important to you—and judge your growth against them.

These benchmarks should be selected with care, because you are going to use them as guidelines to tell you how well your career is advancing. As long as you don't appear overly ambitious, it's fine to discuss your guidelines—as goals—with your superiors. Don't, however, be so specific that you paint yourself into a corner.

If your boss not only supports your goals, but acts to help you realize them, you should be very satisfied. If he doesn't, you should drop back and throw the ball out of bounds: cool it for an extended period, then approach the same objective from a slightly different tack. This may seem unnecessarily devious, or overreaching, but it's not that at all. You are doing nothing more than gently testing the limits of the job. As long as your performance matches your aspirations, you have every right to do so. Your benchmarks should be neither inflexible nor unchanging, but they should be set and used.

Especially irritating is the situation where you work closely with your supervisor—in a mentor relationship, perhaps—and you have received very specific promises about the timing and nature of your advancement. You've kept your end of the bargain; you've been spectacular, but your mentor has not responded. You're concerned that his peers are increasingly viewing you as his flunky, a techno-nerd who can only function in his shadow. Your problem is that their perception may become reality, and if it does, your plans for advancement may be destroyed unless you act. Don't act hastily; be persistent in your efforts to have your responsibilities expanded and to move out from your mentor's shadow. But if after a year of trying you still haven't been successful, consider other options—from transfer to activating your job search.

You may miss the old type of paternalistic corporate loyalty, but if you understand the limits of the new loyalty, you'll enjoy a healthier, more professional relationship with your employer. You're an asset that's been acquired via a rental agreement. It's expected that, as with any asset, a certain rate of return will be earned. As long as it is, the asset may be kept. If it isn't, it may not be sold immediately but it certainly has become disposable. That's the company's view. Your view is its mirror image: I'm an asset that's becoming more valuable, more productive. Is the rate of return I'm earning changing to reflect those improvements?

Loyalty Is a One-Way Street

Finally, as if your life wasn't complicated enough, what if you should find yourself in this situation: You have just moved into one great job when you're offered one that's even better. Would you consider that a dream or a nightmare? It depends on how you handle it.

Remember that an important objective of your job search (more easily sought than achieved) was to generate multiple job offers. Sometimes several offers are made, but not at the same time. It's unlikely that you will know that more than one offer is to be forthcoming; but you do have to respond to the one in hand.

In more concrete terms: You have accepted an offer of a job that overall rated between a "2" and a "3" on your rating scale. You are just unpacking in your new office when another offer is made. Perhaps this is for a job you thought wasn't going to be filled, perhaps it was for a position for which you thought you were no longer being considered. In any event, you're surprised. Moreover, as you learn more about the specifics, you find that you're rating them all "5" or "5+." This truly is the job you've been looking for; it is for real and they want you. Damned if you do, damned if you don't, aren't you? You'll feel like a devious and unprofessional slug if you walk out on your new job now, but you'll always regret it if you don't go. How should you respond?

A good way to decide is to imagine what would happen if the situation was somewhat reversed. Suppose you had accepted an offer, and given notice at your old job, when an edict came down: job freeze! How do you think your case would be handled? Would an exception be made? Would their agreement with you—a letter extending an offer, which you'd accepted—be kissed off with an offer of a modest settlement but without a job?

I think I've made this example clear enough so that your choice should be easy: take the higher rated job. You may offend those at the company where you've just started, and they may be angry enough to try to damage your reputation. But the damage they can do is limited, because in similar circumstances most people would do as I'm advising. You'll hate yourself forever if you don't move on; your career may be set back for years from the level it could otherwise reach. That is the ultimate criterion: Which job is best for my career? The choice may not always be easy, but it should be clear.

CHAPTER ELEVEN

Making the Most of Office Politics

Office politics may have been a non-issue in your last job, or during your job search. You may have paid little attention to internal politics in your last job, but you should recognize now that being oblivious is not a viable option. As you settle into your new position, it's worthwhile to think about how office politics can affect your future success. If you have been a "politician" since the age of seven, when you first talked your older brother into helping you out on your newspaper route, some of this may seem basic. For most people, it is not; it is the most difficult part of their life at work, and the one they comprehend the least.

Your new environment is likely to be more stressful and more competitive than the one you left. It will therefore be easier for you to botch up your interpersonal relationships. And it will be harder to deal with those unpleasant situations that invariably arise and those "bad" people you'll inevitably encounter. So let's review a few basics.

The first thing to do in your first days and weeks on the job is to look and listen; observe as though your life at this company depended on it. Notice how people at all levels relate to each other during the business day. How formal or informal is the environment? Are people on a first-name basis; is it Mr. and Ms. when addressing the more senior levels? Are people treated as human beings and with professional respect, or are some—the newer hires, the more junior people, and the support staff—treated as though they were part of the furniture? Is the atmosphere casual and relaxed or serious and intense?

Can you figure out who sets the overall tone for the office? Is it the senior manager, or is he away so often or locked up in his office so often that it's a senior subordinate who mostly runs things? Whoever it is, who are this person's closest associates? Who do they seem to spend the most time with—is it those directly below them in the hierarchy, or do they relate to colleagues in other departments or farther down in the ranks in your department?

Who are these people who orbit around the central figure? Are they young or old? Do they seem to have the same backgrounds or are they a diverse bunch? What, actually, do these people do?

How do their personalities differ—are there any with a visible sense of humor? With tempers? Who are withdrawn? Gregarious? Sarcastic? Is there a real bastard among them (a self-made man, not an accident of birth, to quote a line from an old movie). If there is, how does this person fit in, and what is his or her particular function? If they don't seem to have a function other than what they normally do, is it possible that they're so good that their personality is simply tolerated?

Who in this group seems to be most interested in you? Do you feel you're relating well to them? Is your immediate superior a "member" of the group? How do the others relate to him or her? Who else on your level interacts often with the group? Are they perceived as rising stars or time-servers?

When you've answered these questions, you can begin to understand the forces in the sea you're swimming in—and whether the temperature of the water pleases you.

The central rule of office politics is don't say anything you'd be embarrassed to have played back to you if it was tape recorded. For instance, you can easily be sucked into the popular game called Let's Trash the Absent Colleague. You may not be able to avoid being in the room when this game is going on, but that doesn't mean you have to be a willing participant. It may be impossible to stay silent, but even if everyone else is piling on, keep your comments completely innocuous. This won't always be easy, because such nasty sport can seem like great fun. It often appears, too, that the person leading the attack is also the most respected, longest-surviving person around. You cannot afford to risk putting yourself on that level. You can nod, smile, and talk in nonsequiturs if you have to, but say nothing else.

That's easier said than done, isn't it? It is difficult to avoid being a participant when the agent provocateur is your boss or a "well-regarded" associate. It doesn't take much to create an office environment in which this kind of relentless nastiness can proliferate; one S.O.B. is usually enough. Such behavior isn't going to be automatically condemned when it's recognized at a higher level. If the provocateur is an exceptional producer, it's not unlikely that they'll tolerate it to a greater degree than they would have been in less demanding times. Nice thought, isn't it? If you complain or decline to participate, you'll be marked as a whiner and a wimp.

If you do feel obliged to get involved, if you ever have felt that way, don't pretend you're getting involved in something inconsequential. Those picked as targets can be worn down and rendered ineffective—and the target could easily be you.

At times you'll have to say something negative about someone, in front of other people. When an honest, open, professional judgment is required as part of your responsibilities, it must be offered. When your judgment is negative, you have to be sure it is fair, professional, and unemotional. You must be prepared to defend it with facts and prepared to accept the fact that not everyone will agree with you.

Engaging in office politics at the personal level can have as much impact on the people being judged as the professional judgments you express about your colleagues or subordinates when asked by your superiors. If you're regarded as a person who has the breadth, subtlety, insight, and sophistication to offer appraisals that are balanced, you'll have accomplished a lot. Caricatures won't be appreciated; recognizably human portraits will.

Another important rule: Never, ever repeat anything you're told. Living by this rule will do more than anything else to establish your reputation for credibility and integrity. Nothing, even trashing someone else, will get you isolated faster in your company than an open-mouth policy. Trashers can be selective. Gossips, by their nature, never are; they are indiscriminate talkers. But you could easily become one if you view sharing information as a way of ingratiating yourself with your new associates.

It shouldn't matter whether or not you were specifically asked not to spread a piece of information. Unless instructed otherwise, there just is no reason to pass it on. Here's how I've tested this concept when I arrived in a new job. I've shared various small bits of information about my background or my interests with my new coworkers. Then I've seen what bits came back to me, and via what routes. That information told me volumes about existing internal grapevines, and about who could be trusted to be discreet and who couldn't.

Is there a decent, productive form of office politics? Sure there is. It involves getting to know, like, and support all those you work with, from the newest receptionist to the top brass. You'd be surprised how many people frown on this practice. They believe in the primacy of the hierarchy, are as rank-conscious as any recent West Point graduate, and believe that communication should be to and through the chain of command. If you are friendly with secretaries other than your own, you're accused of flirting, rather than trying to maintain cordial relationships. Do you and another person who's one level above your boss have mutual interests that you discuss?

That's disloyalty, that's going around your boss. Such concerns are petty and demeaning. You'd like to assume that everyone in the job, regardless of their level, is as dedicated to professionalism in their jobs as you are in yours. If so, you can enjoy their company, respect the professionalism of their work, and develop productive and mutually supportive working relationships.

For you to grow and build a record of accomplishment, you'll need the support of everyone with whom you come in contact—everyone. Not only will you enjoy life more by operating this way, you will open up lines of communication that will help you do your job. You'll learn more, faster, about interpersonal relationships and developing events within the organization than you could by any other means.

Sexual Harassment

How do you pronounce the word *harassment?* That's as simple a question as you will ever have to address in discussing this subject. Everything else is more complicated. Since the confirmation hearings of Associate Justice Clarence Thomas in the fall of 1991, the issue has been front and center on the media stage. Awareness of the problem has been growing as the number of women at all levels in the work force has grown. The coverage of the subject has been interesting if not always enlightening. A prime example of the latter was Helen Gurley Brown's famously fatuous *Wall Street Journal* column in October of 1991 describing life in an office in the 1940s, in which part of the normal routine was chasing women around the office and removing the underpants of those who were caught.

For what it is worth, here is the perspective of a male who has seen the issue coming closer to the surface for several years. It's obvious that the problem exists and in some cases is blatant. But there is a large twilight zone in which it is not possible to see clearly what constitutes proper and improper behavior.

A male who has been a long-term employee of a staid old company in which there were few female professionals may be shocked by what he sees and hears when he moves into a different environment. In the early part of the last decade, working in a large metropolis, some of the foulest and most sexually explicit language I'd ever heard came from the mouths of women executives. In that regard they really weren't that different from any of their male counterparts, because such language was an acceptable part of the corporate culture. Some of it was funny; we worked long hours and there were many times when evening working sessions became extremely informal as we struggled to meet deadlines. Raunchy zingers were then viewed as appropriate tension relievers; they advanced our bonding as a team.

I liked the women behind those zingers, and their choice of language in no way diminished my respect for their professionalism, but there's no way I'd be as sanguine about the appropriateness of such language today—from a male or female, in any business situation.

It is clear that the most prudent approach nowadays is to assume an attitude of professional civility. Does this mean forsaking the raunchy language? Does it mean that if you do you will be regarded as a hopelessly old-fashioned prude? Possibly. It all depends on the situation in the office and the extent to which such language is merely tolerated, as opposed to being widely accepted as normal. It is also clear that polite, civil behavior may be misunderstood. I've gotten dirty looks from female associates when I held open doors for them, and once was asked if I got airsick by a woman when I offered her the window seat on a commuter plane that was about to provide some spectacular low-level views of Manhattan on a flight out of LaGuardia Airport. If you are secure in your beliefs and how they are manifested in your behavior, negative comments shouldn't bother you.

Are there any broadly applicable rules that can always be observed, that will always put you on sure footing? It is hard to say that there are, because what may be considered appropriate and acceptable behavior in the rough-and-tumble environment of an engineering field office may be completely out of place in the more staid setting of a small financial institution. In any event, here are a few ideas to consider.

- In the 1980s, profanity often seemed to be used routinely as punctuation. That doesn't make it any less offensive. It is impossible to assert that rough language isn't offensive "in the context." It may offend some in any context.

- Always think twice before you speak or act. In an effort to get acquainted and feel at ease with new associates, you may be tempted to become more familiar than the stage of development of the relationship warrants. When you are first getting acquainted, watch carefully how people react to your manners; if they don't respond positively, modify your behavior and cool it.

- It is easy to suggest that you can have two sets of standards for behavior: a strict one for everything that takes place in the office, and a more lenient one for anything that takes place away from the office, whether it's at a working dinner or a company picnic. That's a double standard which is unworkable. It's better to have one standard for anyone from work, anywhere.

- It's entirely possible that your concern for appropriate behavior at all times may lead to a breakdown in communications. That needn't happen if you relax and relate to people on the terms that you sense they are most comfortable with.

The concern about sexual harassment is not going to disappear. As long as people try to use power as a weapon or sex as a substitute for skill, problems are going to arise and will have to be dealt with.

Promoting Yourself

"There's no limit to what someone can accomplish, if they don't care who gets the credit."

"Self-praise stinks."

These two phrases, in the context of today's business environment, don't have a great deal of relevance. If you don't promote yourself, who will? Self-promotion, well done, is a healthy way to play office politics well.

The only way your accomplishments are going to be recognized is if you shine a light on them—regularly. Modesty in the workplace can be self-defeating and counterproductive. If you don't make your accomplishments known—connecting the action or the result clearly to the person—you—who was responsible for it, then someone else will get the credit. And if this happens often enough, people will begin to wonder: What's ol' what's-his-name done for us lately?

Promoting yourself doesn't mean divesting yourself of humility. You need humility to survive; it's what keeps you honest about yourself. Modesty, in this context, is a reluctance to step forward into the spotlight. You may be one of the important people in your department, but unless you stand up and stand out, you may eventually be treated as insignificant, no matter how competent you are.

Some events I witnessed several years ago brought this point home to me. A new man in our shop who tried to use our computer system for a project concluded that it had a number of serious deficiencies. He soon learned that others recognized these deficiencies but ignored them. All but the most routine projects were farmed out at considerable expense to computer consultants. He wrote memos on the subject to our boss, who reacted indifferently. So on his own he began seeking solutions, and within six months and with only modest expense he had a new system in operation.

The results were impressive. We gained the ability to take on more complicated projects, and we saved literally hundreds of thousands of dollars by bringing work in-house.

As soon as the results became visible, however, our department head, a master of self-promotion, took over. He began inviting the brass down to see the new system in operation— as demonstrated by him. He told them he had initiated the change, told them how he'd carefully analyzed the problem, made the decision, and then asked the new person to test the system for him! That was the extent of the recognition my friend was given.

Our boss was able to get away with this blatant fraud in plain sight of his peers for one reason: The new guy remained silent. By the time he realized he had been denied the credit he deserved, it was too late. If he had made noise at that point, he would have been perceived as a presumptuous and disloyal subordinate.

The time for him to have acted—the time for you to act— is when you realize you may be accomplishing something significant. You must start talking about it; you can talk to your boss (casually), to the Key Player (see below), to your colleagues. To your boss, you minimize what you think you're about to accomplish. Say things like, "I'm not sure this project is going anywhere," or "Well, there may be some results here, but they're in the future."

Now that is a distinctly different message than you've been giving everyone else, but don't worry. Unless you've made extravagant claims to them, your boss will be too busy to detect the differences in nuance, even if he notices them. Your objective is to keep your boss off the scent of something he may want to take credit for—unless you're confident that he's the type who avoids the limelight and is quite willing to let it shine on his worthy subordinates.

How you publicize yourself is as important as your determination to do it. Too much noise is a turnoff. Far more effective is persistent, low-key promotion, which is almost always in the form of one-on-one contact, talking about what you've accomplished recently, in the context of advancing department or team goals. This promotion has to be done with care and subtlety or it will backfire. But that's a reasonable risk compared to the risk of remaining invisible.

As long as you are performing at a high level, bringing forth accomplishments of substance, you must not neglect self-promotion.

The Key Player

In every organization there is an indispensable individual I call a Key Player. To sustain your recovery, you should have no higher priority than getting as close as possible to this individual.

The Key Player (man or woman) is almost certainly not the CEO or the Chief Financial Officer. Nor is he or she the Old-Timer, the career-dead time server to whom management types pay polite attention but otherwise ignore. If you know how to look, the Key Player is easy to spot; every large enterprise has several of them scattered around. For sure, this person has seniority: at least a decade, for it takes that long to acquire the type of influence he has. The Key Player may hold a staff or a line position, but his influence extends across the organization.

It will be widely agreed that she is a high-level performer, but not a superstar. She will be high up organizationally, but at least one or two layers of management removed from the top, and as close to the top as she is likely to get. Those in the higher echelons will have worked with her for many years. She will be viewed as a quiet, reflective person who does much more listening than talking; who suggests and asks, but never orders. In some rare instances, she may even be an unusually experienced intelligent senior secretary. She will be considered a threat to no one.

And no important decision in the organization will be made without the Key Player's input, which is why you should not ignore this person. Because, whether or not you work closely with him, his opinion of you will affect your career in many ways.

If you think that your reputation as an outstanding performer is enough to keep you hired, perhaps you should reconsider. If you pay no attention to the Key Player because you have no direct reporting relationship, you're making a potentially serious mistake. It's important that the Key Player be aware of you, because if you are to survive the hard times, this person's perception of you must be positive.

It is this point that so many hotshots fail to see and that many otherwise average performers intuitively grasp and thus survive long after they might have been replaced, had they not been so astute.

Top management, of course, values formal performance appraisals, and the best appraisal systems are geared toward enabling managers to give three-dimensional assessments of their subordinates. But, when considering whether to take action toward someone—fire, promote, change assignment, or put into a new career development program—managers do not want to act solely on the basis of these appraisals.

They want to know what this guy is really like. Can he help us all? Can we trust him? Has he really adapted well here? Are we going to feel comfortable growing old with him? To answer these questions they will always turn to the Key Player. And in doing so, they know that they have to answer only one question: Does that person get along with the Key Player?

If that person is you and the answer is yes, you will be set for as long as you want to be. If no is the answer, no matter how good your performance may be, or how agreeable your personality, you will have a very serious handicap.

Assuming you recognize and appreciate the Key Player's

importance, the major question is: How do you cultivate this person without coming across as an obsequious toad? It isn't easy, but there are several things you can do. Begin by studying her carefully. Does she have a sense of humor? Many Key Players do not, and many are offended by on-the-job displays of levity. What are her professional and personal likes and dislikes? How close are they to your own? What do you have in common? If you don't have the opportunity to work for her, in what other ways can you interact?

Your answers should provide you with an outline of a game plan for gaining this person's respect and support. She should be treated with the same interest and courtesy as you would anyone with whom you want to have an effective professional relationship; as mentioned previously, office politics in the best sense. But the Key Player should be a special focus of your attention, and your relationship should be guided by several considerations:

- Whenever possible, seek her advice, but in subtle ways that will make your requests appear natural.

- Never decline her requests. Even if it means doing something you consider menial, or working extra hours, positive responses are essential to the impression you want to create. She may never ask you to do anything, but if she does, don't complain and don't hesitate.

- Never argue with her, even if you have a legitimate professional disagreement. If you can't agree with her, you don't have to say so. Instead, say something like, "That's an aspect I hadn't considered."

- Never talk about her, to anyone, on the job or off, under any circumstances. She may hear about it, and won't appreciate it, because you are neither her boss nor her peer.

These considerations of sensitivity are important because of the Key Player's special role in the organization. She probably feels that she should be Top Dog because she knows so much, but she knows that her career has peaked. Her ego, therefore, is as fragile as it is inflated. Yet even though she may have lacked the ferocious competitiveness needed to reach the top, she is indispensable because she is the one person who has nothing to gain or lose by being utterly candid in her judgments. For all these reasons, the Key Player could turn out to be a valued, helpful friend. The Key Player is an indispensable element in your recovery and career advancement.

CHAPTER TWELVE

Office Politics on Paper: Your Annual Performance Review

If you once thought that office politics were inconsequential and incomprehensible, you probably also underestimated the importance of an event that is just as political but occupies only an hour of your entire working year—your annual performance review. But what happens in that hour will have an impact long after the review is completed, in ways you may not have imagined.

You may be encouraged to believe otherwise. One of my former senior superiors expressed a common perception when I told him of my concern about the way the evaluation process was being conducted. "Hell, Chris," he said, "relax. Everyone here knows those evaluations are a joke. No one takes them seriously."

That is one of the great baldfaced lies you are likely to hear in your business career, because senior management does indeed take them seriously, and does use them for a variety of purposes: who to cut, who to keep; who to advance, who to leave behind; who to reward, who to ignore. So you darn well should take them seriously, too.

This does not mean that the evaluation process is totally serious. Many managers tend to view it as a farce, a ritual that must be dispensed with in as little time as possible. But because it represents your official corporate performance record on paper, you need to pay attention to how the process works, and to what you can and can't do to influence it.

The process of course is political. With management pressured to deal with more important tasks, the evaluation process can become more haphazard and subjective than in any human resources professional's worst nightmare. It is political because it seems that increasing weight in evaluations is being given to factors other than solely technical or professional competence and accomplishments, as those things can be measured. More attention is being given to less tangible factors such as "fit," and that means different things in different corporate cultures. In real life "fit" can even vary within a company.

With so many excellent professionals available today, such intangibles assume increased importance as a means of making selections. That is why it is important to recognize the multi-faceted nature of an evaluation, and why poor performance in one area of your evaluation, which you may have considered minor, can do disproportionate damage to your career.

Does your rating depend on the ratings of others, regardless of your absolute level of performance? To an extent, it does, and it's easier for the ratings of others to adversely impact yours if you are less than an outstanding performer. If you are in fact less than stellar, is there any way to give yourself an edge? There is—by focusing on intangibles, such hard-to-measure attributes as cooperativeness, congeniality, and extended effort, which can all lend a luster to your work that your professional skills may not.

What influence can you realistically expect to exercise over the evaluation process? Not a lot, but some—that is if you recognize the importance of "excellent" or "above-average" ratings and if you focus on how the process works.

This should be another of those objectives about which you get very single-minded: Your objective should be "excellent" in almost all of the rating categories, and no less than "above average" in any category, every year. (It is worth noting, however, that your supervisor may consider one or more categories so ridiculous that almost everyone is given an "average" rating; nothing higher, nothing less.)

Why are "average" ratings so deceptively dangerous and unacceptable? Why can they derail your recovery? "Average" people will never have access to work that is challenging and satisfying. They are likely to be relegated to routinized, repetitive jobs that their peers consider "scut work." Moreover, more companies seem to be adopting a "grow-or-die" or "up-or-out" personnel philosophy, which means that those who haven't demonstrated the ability or the potential for above-average performance will be allowed to wither on the vine or be pruned.

To be sure, there is "grading on the curve," which means that performance is relative. Your rating can vary greatly from one part of the company to another, even though the work is similar, because your competition varies. It is also true that in many places there are those who do hang on year after year with average or even below-average ratings. Such people are kept on primarily because their companies want to avoid the perception of any kind of discrimination. This can work in your favor if you're along in years, but it is still risky. There are too many horror stories of time-servers being let go a year or even a few months before their pension rights would have become vested or maximized. And the genuinely mediocre performers who do hang on are finding that times are tougher. They are learning it's possible to go for years with no "merit" salary increases, no cost-of-living increases, nothing. Increasingly they are subject to actual demotion or transfer to less attractive work. There are no hiding places left.

But you're not looking for a place to hide, you're looking for a place where you can compete successfully and be recognized as a winner. And if, after no more than two years, you haven't convinced your bosses that you're not part of that lump in the middle of the pack, the risk to you will increase greatly.

Consider now the elements of an actual performance review, something you may not have focused on in the past. For each performance category, there are several possible ways you can be graded; the A to F scale and the 0 to 10 scale seem to be common.

The categories might look like these:

1. **"Work Effectiveness."** I've also seen this as "Problem-Solving Ability." This may be the most important category, for it means one thing: Technical Competence.

2. **"Ability to Work Independently," or "Initiative."** The degree to which you are a self-starter who requires little guidance.

3. **"Cooperativeness/Relationships."** The extent to which you actively support various corporate objectives in your work, and develop and maintain effective professional relations with everyone with whom you come in contact.

4. **"Verbal, Written Communications Skills."** Not just a measure of your ability to talk and write clearly and concisely. It's a measure of your ability to listen and synthesize others' ideas as well, to communicate in the manner most appropriate for each audience, and to maintain open communications with all your associates.

5. **"Interpersonal Skills."** Although this may be another way to get your supervisor's perspective on #3, it's also a variation: How well does this person interact with

others in nonroutine situations? Does she/he consistently evidence interest, warmth, and concern when making new contacts? Are difficult interpersonal situations handled tactfully, calmly, intelligently?

6. **"Growth Potential/Potential for Personal Advancement."** Are you interested in acquiring new skills that will help you do your job better and prepare for advanced jobs? Are you interested in learning more about what other people around you do? Are you reasonably obsessed with advancing?

Numerous categories could be added: Exercise of Managerial Skills; Flexibility/Adaptability; Staff Development Skills. These, however, give you a sense of what is involved. But unlike your college midterms, you have no idea how many points out of a possible 100 each question is worth.

I've kept a copy of this evaluation form in my desk wherever I've been. I take it out and review it every three or four months. I grade myself as objectively as I can, and if there are any areas I'm unsure of, I try to get specific feedback, not only from my manager, but from others I work with, at all levels. It's helpful.

After you've been hired for your next job, just before you start and without making too much of an issue, ask for a copy of the appraisal form, and spend 10 or 15 minutes reviewing it. If anything's not clear, ask someone in Human Resources to explain it. Ask, too, which the company considers the most important aspects of your performance, and why. This conversation, just before you step on to the firing line, should serve to clarify the opinions you've formed about what is necessary to succeed. And if the Human Resources' person's perception of what's most important differs from what you have been told by your new boss, obviously pay attention to your superior's perceptions, while concluding, possibly, that you were just getting a largely ignored "official line" from Human Resources.

Even though it may hurt, you may find it illuminating to review your past performance with someone in the company you left. A candid review of the reasons you were let go may be painful, but perhaps not as painful as making the same mistakes again. This may be more than you can bear at an especially difficult time, but such information can be very helpful. Don't be surprised to hear, "Smithers, you're just not cut out for the kind of work you were supposed to be doing." That's bad news, but you would be foolish to ignore it. Or to ignore more moderately modulated messages such as, "A few people here thought you came on a little strong." No kidding? What does THAT mean? A fair translation might be, You roared in like a bull through a china shop and never stopped. In any event, such feedback is free, and can be as valuable as professional tests that you'll pay a lot for.

When you've been an outstanding performer, it's more difficult to believe that any third-party advice could be useful, and you may be right. It's possible that, without changing anything about yourself, you'll do better in a different environment; more structured/less structured, bigger/smaller, any situation in which your few flaws are not as critical as they evidently turned out to be. When interviewing for a new job, you must find out about the performance evaluation process before you accept an offer. If you're used to a formal, structured evaluation process and conclude that the process in the company in question is much less rigid, you'll have to decide how important that is in your overall considerations.

Even though high ratings are very important, there are a very few reasons why it's acceptable to tolerate "average" ratings temporarily. You may be well below the "learning curve" for a particular part of your job, or there may be an aspect of the new corporate culture that you're struggling to adapt to.

You should obviously try to understand why your ratings haven't been higher, but don't expect much help from your immediate superiors. They will expect you to be sensitive enough to understand the situation you are in, simply on the basis of the information they have provided you during the formal performance review, and in the other comments they've made during the year.

You can do several things in a complex work environment to favorably influence your ratings. In an ideal environment you will have, from your first day as a new employee, a clear and specific understanding of what is expected of you on the job: what will be expected of you immediately, what you'll be expected to learn, and what you won't be expected to do. You should have begun to gain that understanding during your first interview, and any points that were left undecided should be settled right now.

You will start out with a set of objectives for the coming year that are as quantified as it's possible to make them; that is, "X number of sales calls, Y number of closed sales," and there will be a thorough understanding of methods and approaches.

Assuming that, finally, you are satisfied that you and your new superiors are speaking the same language, you should expect few misunderstandings about your performance during your first year on the job. If you exceed your objectives, you should get a higher than average rating and have a better than even shot at promotions.

It *should* be that way, but it often isn't. The process will be considerably more complicated, because it will rarely come down just to numbers. The evaluation process is intended to provide a broad overview of your performance, going beyond the purely quantitative aspects. The review and the process are intended to assure a fair, complete, and objective evaluation of each employee, and by measuring performance against previously agreed on objectives, to serve as a tool for their career development. Unfortunately, the results of the process are often the opposite of those intended. The process often is perceived as a sham that has little relation to fairness or objectivity.

Don't expect too much in the way of objective measurement of your performance. This may come as a surprise, particularly if you have a frontline job: you either make the sale or you don't; there's either a closing or there isn't. It's all black and white. Pass or fail. Unfortunately, that's not the way it works in real life. It's so easy for a devious manager to make your accomplishments seem much less real than they are. Consider: You claim you closed a $20 million deal this year? Well, you were our team leader, but our division head and I made some behind-the-scenes contacts before you ever got involved. You don't know how easy you had it. Or, the Catch–22 of the same deal: Well, you closed it, you did the work, but we had to pay out so much in finder's fees that we made virtually no profit on the deal.

There's nothing you can do about such maneuvers and their endless variations, except be prepared to articulate and defend your accomplishments as forcefully as you can. Finally, recognize that it may take time for you and your new bosses to get on the same wavelength. The sooner this happens, the better off you'll be. If after six months you are not finely tuned in, the problem is serious.

Because most supervisors do not like to do annual reviews, and dispense with them as quickly as possible, the details of your rating in each category are likely to consist of episodic recollections of incidents that reinforce the manager's impressions of your performance, which were formed during your first weeks or months on the job. If those impressions are negative, it will be difficult to ever change them. That is why it is so important to discuss performance evaluation policies during the hiring process.

Still, it remains a fact of life: These evaluations aren't fair and never will be. You are stuck with whatever evaluation system your company has, as it has been adapted by its management. What can you do to make the most of it?

Begin by understanding that it's in your interest to get informal feedback on your performance as often as you can during the year, before the formal review, without appearing to be a masochist. The way to do this without giving your boss extra reasons to knock you down if he's so inclined is to simply and casually review with him the way a particular project you were in charge of progressed, emphasizing the positive and highlighting your contributions. Then LISTEN. Listen for his reactions, spoken and unspoken, and probe for responses, but don't push.

When preparing for the annual review, think about what you can do to favorably impact the review. This is not a high-percentage shot, but it's worth taking. Assume you are sitting down for your second annual review. The first one was just Average, you believe this one is going to be Average, and you want to do everything you can to change it to Above Average before you give it up as a lost cause and reactivate the job search.

Listen to your superior make her points, explain the category ratings. Do not respond or react until she has finished. When your turn comes, start off by describing in detail any significant personal accomplishments that may not have been mentioned. It is important to get those things into the record, even if the boss seems reluctant to put them there, because if you have been categorized as less than outstanding, you may not be given credit for significant accomplishments.

Category by category you should make your case for Above-Average ratings. They may be hard to get; you may be pressured to sign off on the Average rating right then and there. You may feel that, having made your points, you have no choice but to do so. But you really should try for a formal reconsideration. If the answer still comes back, "You're Average," then it's time to start off in another direction.

If you remain uncertain about the reasons or justification for Average ratings, it won't hurt to consult with Human Resources, particularly if your next step is activating your job search. This is an open request from you for advice, and you'd better be prepared for a shot to the solar plexus: "Look, I'm glad you finally had the good sense to ask, because you must be the only one who can't see you have no future where you are." This may not be the answer you expected, but take it for what it's worth. It may be said, too, that by this time you should have developed enough smarts, and enough sensitivity that you don't need the insights of a third party to figure out what's going wrong.

Occasionally, however, no matter how savvy you are, you may find yourself utterly at a loss to figure out what's holding you back. They can be truly weird problems, problems that could have been overlooked by the most sensitive person. If you have Above-Average ratings in most categories, it's likely that a knockdown in one area can be a real sore point. Examples I've experienced or learned about:

- You are a morning person, your superior is an evening person, and you are never around when she wants to brainstorm problems; she goes to others who are more accessible when she is in the mood to talk. Result: you get downgraded in one or more categories.

- You like to sit down and informally discuss and resolve issues as soon as they arise. She seeks input from many people, in memo form, and prefers group consensus to settle problems. Her bureaucratic and your informal approaches prevent you from communicating clearly, from understanding what the other wants and needs. Result: more unnecessary negatives.

Trivial? Not if you find out that such trivia is hurting your ratings. Other equally trivial tidbits from third parties may help you in similar situations: "Your boss is very serious. The only time you should ever laugh is when you see him laughing. He's utterly convinced that anyone with a sense of humor is a lightweight." And, "You may not know it, but your boss's oldest, closest buddy is Joe Zipp, and that little run-in you had with Zipp last year didn't help you a bit."

What won't help you is constantly trying to salvage a situation that's beyond hope. First impressions are likely to be the ones that last; if you feel you're the kind who grows on people, and that neutral (average) impressions will change to above average as people get to know you, patience may pay off. You can try the ways suggested here to correct the impressions. Your pride may dictate that you try. But if your efforts don't produce results—higher ratings—in 12 months, take your act someplace else.

CHAPTER THIRTEEN

On Your Own

The title of this chapter can be either a question or a serious suggestion. Some people find the thought of starting their own business terrifying, a harebrained idea that will lead to the loss of everything they own, at the end of a long, exhausting ordeal filled with 80- and 90-hour weeks. For others, the loss of a job presents a once-in-a-lifetime opportunity to *go for it*—to bring to life those ideas for doing things better that they've thought about since they started working. For all of us, the actual or impending loss of a job presents a challenge to see things differently, to recognize that, for better or worse, things are never going to be the same again.

That recognition may strike fear into your heart or it may challenge and inspire you. However it affects you, you have to deal with it; you must understand that from now on you're going to be much more on your own than you ever imagined. This may lead you to cut the cord completely, to start out in an independent business; or it may lead you no farther than a healthy reappraisal of your role as an employee/independent contractor.

Consider two women who went all the way to their own enterprises. The stories of Dominique Raccah and Amy Dacyczyn appeared in the *Wall Street Journal* in the fall of 1991.

Ms. Raccah left her job as head of a research group at an advertising agency to start her own publishing company in 1987. Mrs. Dacyczyn, to supplement her husband's Navy income, in 1990 started a newsletter called the *Tightwad Gazette*, to help others save money the way she had learned to.

Ms. Raccah always wanted to be in publishing, but she could not immediately realize that objective when she got out of school. Remember, if you wish to change from a career you don't like to one you're sure you'll love forever, you may be unable to make the transition in one big step. The experience of Dominique Raccah shows how you can achieve your goal, if you are determined enough.

Her path was not a clear, smooth road. It was not possible for her to acquire all the knowledge needed for success before she began. Problems that were not anticipated turned out to be the hardest to solve. Solutions were devised by innovating and adapting, and in 1991 her company, Sourcebooks, Inc., was outgrowing the space in the family home where it had started. Ms. Raccah started her business with just $40,000 in savings. She did, however, have one other valuable asset: a supportive husband.

The Leeds, Maine-based *Tightwad Gazette* started by Mrs. Dacyczyn has grown in circulation from 1,000 to 50,000 at a yearly subscription price of $12. Her entrepreneurial insight was the idea that others would share her interest in penny-pinching—an interest some might say she carries to ridiculous lengths—and be willing to pay for what she's learned and continues to learn.

Although there's no assurance that these or any other start-up small businesses will enjoy continued success, they do illustrate that there are other roads to independence that don't require the six-figure initial price of a McDonald's franchise. What these women demonstrated was a strong faith in their own ideas, a belief that the service they were developing was needed and could be sold. That faith is essential when considering a new business. But it is also true that that strong faith in your own capabilities cannot be lacking, if you are going to succeed in selling yourself anywhere—to customers or to a new employer.

Here's another important insight. When many of us think of "independent business" we think simultaneously of "franchise"; McDonald's or Midas or any enterprise that comes prepackaged with proven methods for everything from site selection to waste disposal. The two women mentioned in this chapter approached entrepreneuring as you must: as an exercise in packaging and providing services that differ in important ways from similar services offered by competitors.

Whether it is assessing the possibilities of new business ideas or deciding what in your experience and expertise makes you more valuable as an employee than any competitor, the questions are essentially the same. Compared to my competitors, what's unique in my background? Is what's unique also valuable? How can value be added to my assets? What businesses might value them most? What combinations of assets do I have that make me stand out? Law and engineering? Teaching and writing? Finance and quantitative research? Where will these combinations be most valuable? Lacking other "traditional" skills, how do I package (present) and sell my outstanding assets? Can these exceptional capabilities be put to use in my own operations? What niche that no one is presently filling can these capabilities be applied to filling?

Think next about all the other skills you need to be successful in your own enterprise. Talk to people who've gone before you and succeeded. Some had substantial bankrolls when they started, whereas others had virtually nothing. Many went full-time into the new ventures from their first day. Some started their businesses as sidelines. All have similar lessons for you.

Regardless of whether you're thinking of buying a franchise or going out on your own, you must acquire solid information about every aspect of the business you are thinking about:

how the product or service is going to be designed, produced, and sold; how much money and how many people will be required to do all these things; where the money will come from, now and in the future; how costs will be controlled at every stage of the process; and how the product will be marketed.

Then look at each area in more detail: design, production, marketing, finance, personnel management. If you are lacking in the requisite skills in any of these areas, you have to determine that hiring specialists will not make the business economically unfeasible.

It's quite possible that you can have access to all the necessary skills and still fail. A necessary extra ingredient is an obsession, a driving need to succeed. The success of the enterprise must be the most important thing in your life—not the only important thing, just the most important thing. The obsession has to drive you constantly. This doesn't mean you have to be "at the store" 100 hours a week, although for some kinds of business that's almost essential. It means that when you're not actually working, a good part of your brain is still engaged, thinking and analyzing. The obsessed are never satisfied. There is always a way to make a product better or easier to use, safer or less costly to manufacture. There are always better ways to satisfy customers, ways your competitors haven't yet dreamed of.

Your obsession must be directed: directed to details. Remember the accountant's saying: God is in the details. Attention must be paid to all of them; no aspect should be too small to escape the small business owner's attention. Neglect details and the devil will be upon you, in the form of an EPA lawsuit, a delivery that doesn't get made, a service that doesn't meet your quality standards, an associate who steals you blind.

Adaptability is another key ingredient. Could you be as flexible as Ms. Raccah? When—not if—you are confronted with the unknown and the unexpected, will you be able to respond decisively and effectively? How good are you in pressure situations? Do you have to think and act on your feet now? How analytical are you? Do you have formal training in law or economics, or life experience that equips you to recognize crises—to see where the greatest threat lies and where solutions might be found? Or are you a more limited, linear thinker, who can't proceed to the next problem until the one immediately at hand is resolved?

Do you know how to listen to markets? Do you know how to find out and keep up with what your customers are buying, rejecting, would buy if it were a little different, would like changed even though they're buying it now, will insist on in their next order, would like added but only if the price is right, would like you to do besides delivering the product, will have to have next year, five years from now, even if they don't know it now?

Do you enjoy what you have set out to do? Do you delight in it? Does it challenge and engage and fascinate you, and energize you so you can work at it almost to the point of exhaustion? Finally, through your gimlet eye, in the cold mirror of we-can't-kid-ourselves reality, are you the best? Can you convince others that what you are selling is a better value than any competitor's?

If you have been nodding your head in the affirmative since you began reading this chapter, if you have recognized yourself here, then you certainly may want to think more about starting your own business.

But even if such thoughts are far from your mind, let me ask you another question. As you return to life as an employee, to how many of these capabilities and personal qualities do you think you can be oblivious to and still expect to survive past the next blip on the business seismograph?

Do you think you can ever again return to being a narrowly focused specialist, even if you are superb at that specialty? Will that ever again be enough? Isn't it much more likely that to grow and to acquire control, you'll have to expand and hone your interests in the range of business activities beyond those that require your immediate attention? Has your experience shown you, as mine has, the value of having a subspecialty at which you also excel, which you could become engaged in full time should the necessity ever arise?

The central point being made here is that there's an increasingly blurred line between what it takes to succeed as an independent entrepreneur and what is required of an entrepreneur who happens to receive a salary from a larger enterprise. The long-term objective of your recovery should be an environment in which you can function as though you are independent. You should strive to satisfy all the entrepreneur's marketplace tests: the best; value; quality; sensitivity and responsiveness to what your customers want; continuing improvement; awareness of your competitive environment.

The missing element here is enjoyment—deriving enough pleasure from your work so that the necessary obsession becomes a happy, healthy one. When you can add in that ingredient, you will truly have it made. Unfortunately there is no way to find out if you are getting close to that objective unless you actually go out and try different things.

That is one reason why you should no longer view a job as a long-term career, as an end in itself. It should instead be seen as a position that will satisfy certain important objectives on your way to the larger objective. It is for that reason also that part-time sideline ventures may help advance you to your objective. If it's true in your case, as it was for Ms. Raccah, that the objective can't be reached directly with one move, then a sideline business may provide the necessary intermediate step that puts the objective squarely in your sights.

After analyzing all your options, you may be most comfortable working for a salary. You'll get no argument here on that point. At the very least, however, broadening your horizons, expanding your capabilities, and enjoying working at a job to which you can impart some real passions will be satisfying for you. Even if nothing else ever happens, you should be able to see more clearly what your other options are, so that one can be developed into the subspecialty, the fall-back area of expertise that is so essential for your recovery, today and tomorrow.

CHAPTER FOURTEEN

Your Recovery's Financial Floor, I

Why Do I Need This?

Now that you are working again, you are entitled to a long, slow sigh of relief. You've accomplished your main objective—securing a new position that meets most of the qualifications that are important to you. You may think that holding on to that job until you are ready to move on to the next one is your only important priority in the months and years ahead.

If you think that way, however, you'll be limiting yourself to future job-market cycles that you'll be able to ride out better than you have in the past, but not control to the extent you should want to—and can! The key to this higher degree of control, to making a large measure of your recovery irreversible and subject only to your direction, is the accumulation of wealth. Even a modest accumulation can give you control you never imagined—and a modest accumulation is well within your reach.

I know, I know; I can hear the sighs of boredom and exasperation rising up now:

- To heck with accumulation; we've been depriving our-
  selves for months. We want to spend!

- Anything related to financial matters bores me to tears.
  I'm too old to acquire any financial expertise now, and
  besides, I don't have any spare time!

- Give me a break! The kind of accumulation you're talking about simply isn't possible for anyone making less
  than a six-figure salary! There's no point in even trying!

Those attitudes are understandable, but taken together they
add up to defeatism and despair. Considering what you've just
come through, how can anyone have as little hope about what
can be achieved in the future?

Look what you've just accomplished: In a brutally competitive job market, you were able to prevail! You acquired skills
that are beyond many people. You learned how to sell yourself, in writing and in person. You've learned things about
yourself and working situations that should increase your
chances of survival in any future job. None of that was easy
or painless, but aren't the results worth it? No pain, no gain
is trite but fundamental.

Nothing I'm going to take you through in the next two
chapters is as difficult as what you've been through. It will be
very new to many of you, but rest assured I am not going to
immerse you in so much detail that you'll think you're being
qualified to become a Merrill Lynch account executive. That
would be way beyond the scope of this book.

I am going to outline how you can learn what you need to
know. Then I'll show you what the possibilities are. Once you
see exactly what you can do, I hope your appetite will be
whetted and that you'll want to accumulate more knowledge,
information, and wealth. Then you'll see that learning how to
shift spending forward to the future—investing—is as much
fun in its own way as spending now. And you will begin to
appreciate that investing for your future in this way is just as

important as what you've done thus far to invest in yourself and your recovery.

Earning and Spending

As you developed your recovery plan and moved it to a successful conclusion, few things may have been farther from your mind than long-term financial planning. Then and now, you may think you need do little more to secure your financial future than to make sure you are vested in a nice pension plan, make the maximum contribution in your 401(k) plan, pay off your mortgage, and make modest additional investments after your kids' college educations have been paid for.

That's certainly the traditional way of looking at financial security. It was a reasonable perspective back in the days when corporate careers could more safely be measured in decades than in years. It makes much less sense today, when frequent job changes may be both inevitable and desirable.

One rationale for spending your entire career in one place has been the pot of gold at the end of the rainbow—the pension plan. A reasonable plan was one that, combined with Social Security benefits, would give you 50 percent of your income upon retirement at age 65 with 30 years of service. How many people do you know who have made it to 30 years with one company and would do it that way again? Would you? Do you think that decision will be yours? I'd like you to consider some other options, all of which lead to something called *financial independence*.

That term has a different meaning for everyone. For some people, it means having enough assets so that they can live off their earnings without working at all. In other words, complete retirement. For others, it means accumulating enough investments to provide for a certain percentage of current income, 50 percent for instance, so that they have much more freedom to choose when and where they'll work, and what they'll work at. For these folks, permanent retirement to a rocking chair on a veranda overlooking a golf course holds no attraction. Their interest is in staying active, at a pace they can control and moderate as they grow older.

To achieve these degrees of financial independence will require a financial plan that you think through as carefully as you did your career plan—and stick to as tenaciously. If you want to avoid the feast-or-famine lifestyle that the changing U.S. business climate may force on you, it's essential that you have such a plan.

Your plan's outline is simple. Your objective is to earn as much income as possible as quickly as you can; to spend as little of it and invest as much as possible; and to make investments that balance risk with growth to produce long-term wealth.

Let's discuss the earning part first. This part has two elements: bringing the dollars in, and dispensing them wisely. A maximum effort plan means that in a two-adult household, there will be at least a 2½-job income stream—two full-time jobs and one part-time job—regardless of whether there are any children. This reduces the risk that both of you will be between jobs at the same time. That part-time job should be taken on with a view to its potential as an alternative full-time career, that second specialty that is so important. This is where career and financial planning come together.

It doesn't matter much what your occupations are now, provided you both have long-term plans for developing your careers. Nor is it critically important for both spouses to work uninterruptedly for the next 30 years. Time off is entirely appropriate, for school or for full-time parenting, as long as the objectives are kept in focus: career growth, earnings growth and, more often than not, 2½ jobs.

Next in importance is intelligent spending. This requires constant attention, to everything from paying the least for necessary goods and services, to clipping discount coupons from the Sunday newspaper. Living frugally and setting aside more for investing than you ever thought possible do not mean committing yourself to a life of deprivation, without luxury, joy, or occasional spending binges. You must, however, become a fanatic about getting the most value for every dollar you spend, and there are more ways to stretch dollars than you ever imagined. The place to start learning is in your nearby bookstore or local library. Many books are available on the subject of personal finance, and in them you can find many useful ideas. A word of caution here: Every prescription is not going to work for every family. Every recommendation should be carefully analyzed to see if it can be used without exposing your family to unnecessary risks or hardships.

What any good personal finance book will lead you to do, however, is something very much worth doing: Examine every aspect of your finances to see if you are getting the most for what you spend, on everything from food to housing to insurance. Many of the changes prescribed will require significant shifts in the way you spend, which is, of course, what is intended. It's obvious that this kind of self-instilled discipline can sometimes be painful, but as the saying goes, "No pain, no gain." If you're willing to be a bit flexible, it's possible you can save a bundle.

Let me use two of my favorite examples to show you what I mean. The two areas where families waste thousands of dollars that could be spent elsewhere or invested are medical care and automobiles. With more families being started later these days, the medical expenses involved in having babies— often many hundreds of dollars of out-of-pocket expenses— can arise at awkward times. That's true even if the parents are covered by a "good" company medical plan, because even the best plans are hitting their beneficiaries with increasingly higher deductibles.

Here is one way to avoid this and other health care expenses: Join a Health Maintenance Organization. A good HMO can reduce your out-of-pocket medical expenses by 90 to 95 percent, because most HMOs have very low deductibles; $5.00 per office visit or procedure is common.

There are disadvantages to an HMO, however. The one we hear the most about is the limited freedom to choose your own physician. Any such limitation may be hard for some families in their child-rearing years to accept, but before you reject the idea of an HMO, you should understand that there are different kinds of HMOs. In a "group model" HMO, all the organization's physicians are employees. When you join, you have to choose from among the employed doctors. In the Individual Practice Association HMO individual physicians, who aren't employees of the HMO, agree to provide services to the HMOs members for a fixed annual fee, the same as with the group model HMO.

For you, the consumer, an IPA-HMO usually means a wider choice of physicians and locations; a greater chance, in other words, of finding a doctor you relate to well, while still realizing the savings of HMO membership.

I wasn't pleased with my first HMO experience. It was a group model, and I found the group's offices crowded and impersonal. For the last seven years I've been with an IPA-HMO, and I'm generally satisfied with it. The occasional office visits are much more pleasant, and the savings have been real and substantial.

Managed health care plans like HMOs are growing in importance as the businesses that offer them, together with other health insurance options, seek ways to reduce their outlays. Employees are finding out that staying away from managed care is an increasingly expensive option.

Another item on which many people waste huge amounts of money is automobiles. Buying a new car every three or four years or 50,000 or 70,000 miles can be a tremendous waste of money—an unnecessary expenditure if there ever was one. Since most of us need cars, the only way to come out even or slightly ahead, and to free up money for other investments as a result, is to pay cash for a car, and then keep it forever! Forever? Darn near: well beyond 100,000 miles and long after depreciation has ceased to be a major cost of ownership. As this is written there are two 8-year-old cars in my garage. One has 133,000 miles on it, the other 151,000, and both are running strong: interiors are in good shape, very minor rust, no oil burning. We have kept them that long because we have maintained them like taxicabs.

With serious attention paid to preventive maintenance of the body, interior, and mechanicals, good modern cars will last for many years. There is one exception to this long-life rule that I think is becoming more important. Modern cars grow more complex almost daily, and I think this complexity is overwhelming the capacity of some dealer service organizations to cope. Therefore, if you do get a lemon, you may well be in for major hassles. If this concerns you, then leasing, not owning, can be an attractive option.

The required preventive maintenance for a car you own and intend to keep isn't cheap, but it is exceptionally cost-effective. Preventive maintenance means keeping the inside and outside in like-new condition, and following the maintenance interval recommendations in your owner's manual, with one critical exception. The exception is: You should change your engine oil and filter twice as often as the manufacturer recommends. In other words, every 3,000 to 4,000 miles. That's the biggest single contribution you can make to your engine's longevity, and that's the main reason why taxicab engines can run so long between overhauls. One of the limo drivers our company uses has a big sedan with 189,000 miles on it, and no work has ever been done on the engine.

Except for oil changes you can do almost everything yourself. There are franchises throughout the country that provide fast oil changes. For what the franchises give you, they are outrageously expensive. I've found local garages using brand-name products that undercut the franchises' prices by 30 to 50 percent. The main thing, however is to get those oil changes done.

Assuming an aggressive schedule of preventive maintenance, is there any reason ever to get rid of your car? There is certainly the possibility you may not have to; 300,000 miles and 15 or 20 years of driving is not out of the question; unusual, to be sure, but not impossible. But you will have to ask yourself, do I really like this car enough to be able to live with it that long? If that is what you plan to do, set up a more intensified schedule of preventive maintenance, including professional exterior and interior cleaning, and regular replacement of other parts such as hoses. And bear in mind that at least once in this long life, you'll have to bear the expense of a rebuilt engine.

When buying, start off with the biggest car you can afford, so you won't have to trade up as your family grows. Get the April issue of *Consumer Reports* magazine (it's their annual auto issue) and check the Frequency of Repair records of cars you're interested in. These records, tabulated by Consumers Union from subscriber surveys, are the best source of information on the mechanical reliability of various automobiles available to the general public. Getting a car that's historically been relatively trouble free can save you many expensive repair bills that aren't covered by warranty.

Should you buy new or used? Unless you drive many miles every year—20,000 or more—there's no reason to pay an outrageous price for a new car. Let somebody else pay for those first 12 or 24 months of depreciation. Your first choice in a used car should be one that, whether it's a year or two old, has fewer than 20,000 miles on it and was owned by a major car rental company. That way, even if you buy it from a new car dealer, you can see the car's maintenance records. If the model you like had (according to *Consumer Reports*) one or more major trouble spots, see if there's evidence of the problem in the maintenance records. If you're concerned that any repairs are likely to be a major expense once the car's out of warranty, find out if you can purchase a reasonably priced extended warranty. If you're still concerned, look at other models.

Is there any justification for buying a new car, other than being a high annual mileage driver who needs to have the car under warranty for as many miles as possible? Sure: You are at the other extreme—you're a very low mileage driver—5,000 to 10,000 miles a year or less. Then you may decide to buy that new car, knowing it's likely to be the last car you'll ever own. And if this is coupled with a burning desire to own all the latest technology, such as multivalve engines and antilock brakes, then you have made a strong case for buying new.

Keep in mind, however, that this technology will cost you more when you buy it and cost more to have repaired. Maybe a lot more, because many independent garages can't or won't service the technologies. For better or worse you may be stuck with the new car dealer's service department.

Should you buy or lease? There is no best answer. I refer you once again to your local bookstore, to see what's been written on the subject. I recently bought a book I've found to be very useful, *The AAA Car Buyer's Handbook*. It has an excellent analysis of leasing versus buying, and much other useful information about selecting your next automobile.

Owning a satisfactory automobile and maintaining it over many years can save thousands of dollars year in and year out. Those savings, or a good part of them, can be spent on assets that don't depreciate, and, of course, a good chunk of the savings should be invested.

Back to Your Budget

Medical care and automobiles are just two examples of how your available funds can be made to work harder for you. All the other ways that you have learned about should be embodied in a plan for weekly, monthly, and yearly expenditures, otherwise known as a BUDGET. Remember that Transition Budget you put yourself on back in Chapter Three? That's a great place to start with your permanent budget.

This expenditure plan should be as controlling in your life as it is for a business. Any deviations from it, above a previously agreed upon amount, should require consent of both partners. More than a few deviations a year should cause you to reconsider (a) how realistic the budget was to begin with, and (b) how much willpower you both have.

There's one test of your willpower that can't be fudged: the amount of your credit card debt. If you have any such debt, and can't quickly and permanently get rid of it, you're going to have major, perhaps insurmountable, problems achieving financial independence. The notion of paying 15 to 19 percent interest rates, even for a month or two on unpaid balances, is something that is not acceptable to anyone who is serious about financial planning. Use the credit cards only for what you know you can afford to pay off completely that month. Forget about anything above that limit.

Another financial folly is the use of home equity loans, for anything other than a home improvement your realtor assures you will increase the value of your home by at least what it cost.

If you compulsively use these gimmicks regularly, you're just kidding yourself if you ever think you'll be able to get off the financial treadmill. What you are doing is exactly the opposite of what you must do to achieve any degree of financial independence: instead of shifting income from the present to the future by saving and investing, you're using future income—loans you must pay back—to pay for current expenditures. For a house that's acceptable. In genuine emergencies, of course, it's okay. For anything else, it should be absolutely out of bounds.

When reviewing all the priorities in a budget, it's often impossible to see beyond your present situation. So when all else fails, try guilt: If you don't make the decision to set aside a significant percentage of your income for investing, you will always regret it. Besides, once the decision is made, it is incorporated into your lifestyle, and it doesn't have to be made again. And there is one painless way to ensure that the amount set aside for investing grows regularly. Decide now that at least half of any raises will be set aside for investing. Most of the remainder can be added for current expenses, and some can be set aside for pure luxuries.

Another "painless" way to accumulate funds for investment is through an employer-sponsored 401(k) plan. This savings plan is far and away the best fringe benefit offered. The availability of a 401(k) should be a major consideration in deciding whether to accept an offered job. A 401(k) plan enables you to invest "pretax" dollars, up to a $7,500 per year limit, which your employer can match—up to a dollar-for-dollar match (which few companies do). The pretax accumulation means that your contribution is deducted, up front, from your taxable income. And your contributions, the company's matching contribution, and the earnings on your investments accumulate tax free.

Usually you'll be offered a choice of investment vehicles, which may include company stock, government stock, and a diversified stock portfolio. If all the funds are invested in a stock portfolio producing a 10 percent annual increase, and your company provides a dollar-for-dollar match, the return on your investment will be 20 percent annually. This is one fringe benefit you cannot afford not to participate in, to the maximum permitted. In the next chapter, we'll show you, in dollars and cents, how such investments can increase in value over time. The results may surprise you.

Spending smart is a rewarding game that should be challenging and fun. Investing smart presents a different set of challenges, and that's what we'll zero in on next.

CHAPTER FIFTEEN

Your Recovery's Financial Floor, II

Investing

There's good news and bad news about investing:

- It is an incredibly complex field; even a full-time professional can only hope to master a portion of it, over a lifetime of work. But, it's not necessary to be a professional to achieve success as an investor.

- There's an overwhelming amount of information that has to be acquired and analyzed, but much of the information you need has been digested for you and is readily available in formats almost anyone can understand.

- There will be times when you need individualized advice; unfortunately, some advisers are charlatans. However, if you apply a few basic, commonsense principles and stick to them, you should be able to find an adviser who's personalized and also reliable.

• There are so many alternatives to choose from; it's extremely difficult for a novice to choose alternatives with the appropriate balance of risk and reward. Difficult, yes; impossible, no. This is, after all, a recovery book. It's recognized that most of your attention will be focused on rebuilding and advancing your career. You're going to be shown, therefore, what kind of investment results are possible with a narrowly focused set of investment objectives that do not require excessive amounts of your time.

Your first investment objective should be to buy the single-family home that is your primary residence. In most parts of the country, single-family home values have held up better in the current housing slump than condominium or co-op prices.

How much down? How long a mortgage? Only partial answers are possible. Enough down to qualify for the lowest interest rate your lender has available. A long enough term so that the monthly payment will not strangle you; you don't want to feel house poor.

It's becoming more obvious every day that houses generally aren't as good investments as they were up through the mid-1980s. They can't be counted on to increase in value faster than the rate of inflation, or outperform other investments. And, with lower personal income tax rates, they are not the good tax shelters they once were. But there aren't many tax shelters left.

Still, all things considered, a house is worth owning and borrowing for. Slow but steady appreciation is likely over the long term, and the interest on your mortgage and your property taxes is still deductible from your federal income tax.

Unless you are talented enough to build your house, buy the newest house you can afford, even if it means a somewhat smaller house. Repairs on older houses, those in the 10- to

20-year-old range, can quickly become major expenses, and won't add to the value of the house when it's sold. Your investment in the American Dream should be enjoyed; it shouldn't become a burden.

There's one more matter to be covered before we get into investing to sustain your recovery over the long term: investing for your kids' college educations. The best investment you can make for this purpose is long-term, zero-coupon, tax-exempt municipal bonds. With these bonds, as with U.S. Savings Bonds, a given amount invested today results in a payout of a known amount at a specified time in the future. Your interest rate is locked in on the date of purchase, there is no federal income tax liability, and you can calculate how much you'll have to invest at the beginning to provide the money you'll need to pay the bursar during Freshman Week in the next century.

One caveat: with today's lower interest rates, some may argue that a good stock mutual fund, even though its price may swing more widely, is likely to produce better results over a 15- to 18-year period than available zero-coupon bonds. The risk to you is that one of those swings may put your principal way down precisely at the time you need it to pay tuition and residence bills.

In investing for your financial floor, for the degree of financial independence you and yours want most, the assumption we're making is that you won't need the money on a certain date in the future, but that you'll be satisfied if your objectives are realized within a reasonable period after a targeted date. In other words, you are investing now for the long haul; you will not be concerned about daily, weekly, or monthly changes in the value of your investments, as long as the average annual rate of growth meets your objectives.

But before thinking about how best to meet your objectives, you need to start educating yourself about personal investing. The place to start is with two publications: *Money* magazine is an excellent source of elementary education in personal wealth acquisition. It is recommended because it educates as well as informs. It's a fine source of information about many types of investments, but its emphasis is on stocks, mutual funds, and bonds.

As a monthly, *Money* magazine provides tables showing how many different mutual funds and other types of investments are performing. A particular strength is its ability to put investment strategies in human terms, with real-world examples, so that readers can compare the techniques and results of others with their circumstances and goals. *Money* can also be lightweight and repetitive, but for the serious investor just starting out, there is nothing better.

The *Wall Street Journal,* which at one time referred to itself in advertising, redundantly, as "the daily diary of the American dream," is as indispensable in its way as *Money* is in its. The columns entitled "Your Money Matters" are consistently substantive and informative. I recommend that you clip these articles and save them in a scrapbook. Moreover, the *Journal's* listings of mutual funds, as well as other investments, are much more comprehensive and current than those in *Money.* Other useful educational information can be gleaned by reading the Explanatory Notes and Footnotes at the beginning of the *Journal's* table entitled "New York Stock Exchange Composite Transactions." *Money* mostly lists just the top 10 or 15 performing mutual funds in most categories, which is fine for many uses; the *Journal* lists all of them.

If you're lucky, your local newspaper carries one of the excellent syndicated financial columnists. The best in my book is the veteran Bill Doyle. I keep most of his columns. In addition to his lucid explanations of investment questions most of us are concerned about, he is a master of uncomplicated expositions on such complicated investments as collateralized mortgage obligations (CMOs). Doyle has common sense and is always to the point.

Also worth reading is Jane Bryant Quinn. She ranges further

afield than Doyle does, but whether she's talking about spending shrewdly or prudent investing, she deserves your attention. If your local cable service provides CNBC, or if your radio carries a Mutual Network station, the Dolans are worth listening to. They're seasoned, skeptical pros with great range and good advice.

You have to become knowledgeable in the basic language of finance and personal investing, and you must keep current. This can be annoyingly time consuming if your investments are highly diversified in such areas as individual stocks and bonds and other instruments. That is why, for the main thrust of your financial recovery, a narrow investment focus is recommended.

It's almost never too late to begin investing. You can't get rich overnight, that's true; the time horizons we're talking about here extend out to 10 and 20 years. But as you'll see, even 10-year results aren't bad and not impossible to realize, given a halfway decent business climate. So even if you are past 40 or 50, start now!

While you may want to diversify your investments as you learn more about investing, the suggestion here is that you work toward financial independence with one type of investment: diversified stock mutual funds. There is a tremendous array of such funds to choose from, and many have been in business long enough so that their track records can be checked back over 10 or 15 years.

In order to give you some idea of the growth potential in long-term mutual fund investments, I've included several tables that track growth in assets for periods of up to 25 years.

Table A assumes your average annual salary over the period is $45,000; 7 percent of it fully matched by the employer is invested in a 401(k) plan in which your investments appreciate at 12 percent a year. Few people would consider a person whose 25-year average annual salary is $45,000 highly paid.

Even at that level, however, it's possible to come close to accumulating a million dollars in 25 years.

TABLE A

ASSUMPTIONS:

Salary		$45,000
Percent invested in 401(k)		7%
(matched by company)		
Investments appreciate at		12%

1	$7,056	14	$228,562
2	$14,959	15	$263,046
3	$23,810	16	$301,667
4	$33,723	17	$344,923
5	$44,826	18	$393,370
6	$57,261	19	$447,630
7	$71,188	20	$508,402
8	$86,787	21	$576,466
9	$104,257	22	$652,698
10	$123,824	23	$738,078
11	$145,739	24	$833,703
12	$170,283	25	$940,804
13	$197,773		

Table 1 makes the following assumptions: Your average annual salary during the period is $60,000; 7 percent of it is invested in a 401(k) plan, fully matched by the employer, and the investments appreciate at 12 percent per year. The investment vehicle is the diversified stock portfolio, in other words, the company sponsored stock mutual fund. It takes just 12 years for the accumulation to exceed a quarter of a million dollars; in 18 years, it passes half a million; and by year 24, it has exceeded a million.

TABLE 1

ASSUMPTIONS:

Salary	$60,000
Percent Invested in 401(k)	7%
(matched by company)	
Investments appreciate at	12%

1	$9,408	14	$304,750
2	$19,945	15	$350,728
3	$31,746	16	$402,223
4	$44,964	17	$459,898
5	$59,768	18	$524,493
6	$76,348	19	$596,841
7	$94,917	20	$677,869
8	$115,716	21	$768,622
9	$139,009	22	$870,264
10	$165,098	23	$984,104
11	$194,318	24	$1,111,605
12	$227,045	25	$1,254,405
13	$263,698		

Table 2 uses the same assumptions as Table 1, with one change. Now, instead of the average annual salary over the 25-year period being $60,000, that is the salary in the first year, and it increases at 4 percent annually thereafter. Now you reach half a million almost two years sooner, and you pass a million in year 21, rather than in year 24.

TABLE 2

ASSUMPTIONS:

Salary	$60,000
Percent invested in 401(k)	7%
(matched by company)	
Investments appreciate at	12%
Annual salary increase	4%

1	$9,408	3	$32,936
2	$20,321	4	$47,471

5	$64,173	16	$500,672
6	$83,320	17	$578,373
7	$105,223	18	$666,104
8	$130,230	19	$765,095
9	$158,733	20	$876,728
10	$191,171	21	$1,002,549
11	$228,038	22	$1,144,294
12	$269,885	23	$1,303,905
13	$317,334	24	$1,483,562
14	$371,079	25	$1,685,705
15	$431,900		

Tables 3 and 4 are the same assumptions as Tables 1 and 2, except that the base salary is assumed to be $75,000 rather than $60,000. The results are equally impressive.

TABLE 3

ASSUMPTIONS:

Salary	$75,000
Percent invested in 401(k)	7%
(matched by company)	
Investments appreciate at	12%

1	$11,760	14	$380,937
2	$24,931	15	$438,409
3	$39,683	16	$502,779
4	$56,205	17	$574,872
5	$74,709	18	$655,617
6	$95,435	19	$746,051
7	$118,647	20	$847,337
8	$144,644	21	$960,777
9	$173,762	22	$1,087,830
10	$206,373	23	$1,230,130
11	$242,898	24	$1,389,506
12	$283,806	25	$1,568,006
13	$329,622		

TABLE 4

ASSUMPTIONS:

Salary	$75,000
Percent invested in 401(k)	7%
(matched by company)	
Investments appreciate at	12%
Annual salary increase	4%

1	$11,760	14	$463,849
2	$25,402	15	$539,875
3	$41,169	16	$625,840
4	$59,338	17	$722,967
5	$80,216	18	$832,630
6	$104,150	19	$956,369
7	$131,528	20	$1,095,910
8	$162,787	21	$1,253,187
9	$198,416	22	$1,430,368
10	$238,964	23	$1,629,882
11	$285,047	24	$1,854,453
12	$337,357	25	$2,107,132
13	$396,668		

Two qualifications should be mentioned, however. In the preceding tables as in those that follow, a smooth upward progression is shown; that's what's meant by the 12 percent average annual increase. In real life, however, it isn't smooth, it's irregular. Also, no one can assure that the good performance of some mutual funds during the last 10 to 15 years is going to be matched over the next 25 years. If you think some other vehicles are going to perform better in the future, that's where you should put your investments. But the past isn't necessarily a bad indicator of what the future's going to be like.

I'm not suggesting that you put these dollars away in the mutual funds of your choice and forget about them. If clear evidence accumulates within enough time for it not to be an aberration, that a fundamental shift in the value of investment vehicles is underway, then you will want to shift, too. Just don't let the headlines scare you. That huge drop in the Dow Jones Industrial Average trumpeted from the front page may, in percentage terms, be only 1 or 2 or a few percent.

Now consider four more tables. This time, straight investments; no matching. This is what you might do on your own with mutual funds, without the benefit of a 401(k) plan.

Table 5 assumes you start out investing $5,000 per year, and that you increase that amount by 4 percent each year, still investing it in our good old 12 percent mutual fund. Even without the leverage of the 401(k) plan, you could get to more than $250,000 in the fifteenth year, exceed half a million in year 20, and pass the million mark in the twenty-fifth year.

TABLE 5

ASSUMPTIONS:

Amount invested	$5,000
Investments appreciate at	12%
Annual investment increase	4%

1	$5,600	14	$220,881
2	$12,096	15	$257,084
3	$19,604	16	$298,019
4	$28,256	17	$344,270
5	$38,198	18	$396,490
6	$49,595	19	$455,414
7	$62,632	20	$521,862
8	$77,518	21	$596,756
9	$94,484	22	$681,127
10	$113,792	23	$776,134
11	$135,737	24	$883,073
12	$160,646	25	$1,003,396
13	$188,889		

Table 6 is the same as Table 5, except that you start off investing a higher amount—$6,250 per year instead of $5,000. This points up the real impact a higher initial level of investment can have, over time. The cumulative impact is most graphically seen at the end: In year 25 you wind up with a quarter of a million more, all because of your initial decision to put an additional $1,250 into the kitty each year.

TABLE 6

ASSUMPTIONS:

Amount invested	$6,250
Investments appreciate at	12%
Annual investment increase	4%

1	$7,000	14	$276,101
2	$15,120	15	$321,354
3	$24,506	16	$372,524
4	$35,320	17	$430,337
5	$47,748	18	$495,613
6	$61,994	19	$569,267
7	$78,291	20	$652,327
8	$96,897	21	$745,945
9	$118,105	22	$851,409
10	$142,240	23	$970,168
11	$169,671	24	$1,103,841
12	$200,808	25	$1,254,245
13	$236,112		

Tables 7 and 8 show what might be achieved in the future by making riskier investments, specifically in a mutual fund appreciating at 15 percent a year rather than 12 percent. There are funds available that have such records over several years, and I hope they continue to produce those results for the next 20 years, because I'm invested in a couple of them. The 15 percent increase, in fact, was the average increase of all stock mutual funds in 1990.

TABLE 7

ASSUMPTIONS:

Amount invested		$5,000
Investments appreciate at		15%
Annual investment increase		4%

1	$5,750	14	$279,347
2	$12,592	15	$331,206
3	$20,701	16	$391,243
4	$30,274	17	$460,699
5	$41,541	18	$541,004
6	$54,768	19	$633,803
7	$70,259	20	$740,988
8	$88,365	21	$864,735
9	$109,489	22	$1,007,548
10	$134,096	23	$1,172,307
11	$162,722	24	$1,362,325
12	$195,982	25	$1,581,413
13	$234,585		

TABLE 8

ASSUMPTIONS:

Amount invested		$6,250
Investments appreciate at		15%
Annual investment increase		4%

1	$7,187	8	$110,456
2	$15,741	9	$136,861
3	$25,876	10	$167,620
4	$37,842	11	$203,402
5	$51,927	12	$244,977
6	$68,460	13	$293,231
7	$87,824	14	$349,184

15	$414,008	21	$1,080,918
16	$489,053	22	$1,259,435
17	$575,873	23	$1,465,384
18	$676,255	24	$1,702,906
19	$792,253	25	$1,976,766
20	$926,234		

These tables should provide an appreciation of the possibilities of steady investments in vehicles that aren't extremely risky. The investor whose primary concern is the preservation of principal at all times may stay far away from stock mutual funds, and instead consider various U.S. government obligations. But, even with those kinds of investments your principal is at risk to inflation. That's why some equity investments are appropriate and even necessary for every stage of your life.

Having seen how it may be possible to acquire reasonable wealth, you should think about how to keep it.

At some point, when your financial obligations have been satisfied, you should become completely debt free. If your house isn't entirely paid off, sell it and buy one you can afford to pay cash for. Some experts say you should always have a mortgage as a tax shelter, a mortgage you can handle with your income, whatever it is.

That's dangerous advice to anyone approaching senior-citizenhood, because of the possibility of catastrophic medical expenses as you grow older. The financial "nut" you have to crack—the monthly expenses you must meet—should go down as your years go up. As you approach retirement, or reduce the amount of time you work, you should start shifting from investments that emphasize growth into less risky investments, including fixed-income assets, that provide a steady stream of income. Investing for wealth should always be a priority, to expand your asset base and to hedge against inflation. But as your working career winds down—whether that happens when you're 50 or 80—risky investments should no longer be your first priority.

A few more points on investing. Suppose you have some extra funds and you want more personalized advice than you get from the media. Where are you going to get it? You can always seek financial advice from the nearest local office of a major national brokerage house. The problem is, it isn't the kind of financial advice you need most. What "financial advice" you will get there is advice that's consistent with the company's generation of commissions from regular transactions; but you are a buy-and-hold investor. Unless the branch manager sees the potential for a sizable steady flow of commission dollars, you aren't going to get close to the more senior brokers in the office, who may be able to offer insights worth paying for.

You can also obtain financial advice from professionals who work full time at personal financial advising, who don't do it as a sideline as do some accountants and lawyers. The problem here, as with the brokerage houses, is that you'll need a sizable amount of money to begin with in order to gain access to the best talent. And, they may slant their advice to get you to invest in products on which they earn a commission.

There are, however, advisers who work on an hourly basis and don't receive commissions on investments. They don't necessarily have to take over the active management of your assets to provide you with advice. If you're considering this kind of adviser, you must check their performance record. Get the names of active clients they've been serving for at least five years (less than that isn't long enough for a fair test), and then talk with them. Are the other clients' objectives the same as yours? If not, look for another adviser whose clients have objectives more in keeping with your requirements. How has this adviser performed over time—what's $1,000 invested with this person over 5 or 10 years worth now? Compare this number to some benchmark, such as *Money* magazine's top-ranked "All Weather" mutual funds. If this adviser hasn't outperformed those funds, you should seriously consider if you need an independent adviser at all.

You may be tempted periodically to consider investments other than the diversified stock mutual funds that should play the dominant role in your financial recovery. You can easily find people willing to sell them to you—through the mail, over the radio, or through "investment seminars." If you want to dabble in these investments occasionally, by all means, do so. But initially, only with money you can afford to lose. If they happen to work out well for you, use them as an alternative to mutual funds.

What About Real Estate?

For years some of the most popular business books on the market were about real estate investing. They promoted paths to riches with "no money down" and using "other people's money." They were best-sellers in the 1980s. But how attractive is real estate as an investment in the 1990s? Your own home is still a good investment, but beyond that, investing in this sector doesn't make as much sense for most people as it did it the past.

Real estate still has undeniable attractions, the primary one being "leverage." This means you get control of a valuable asset for a down payment that's a fraction of its value, and you get all of any appreciation in value. The numbers can be appealing. You buy a $90,000 piece of real estate for 15 percent down, or $13,500. In two years, you sell for $97,344, assuming a 4 percent annual appreciation. You've made a cool $7,344 profit, not a bad return on $10,000 for two years. And this return doesn't take into account other possible benefits, such as depreciation.

Nor, unfortunately, does this example give a complete picture of the costs and risks. You can easily incur $3,000 in transaction costs buying your $90,000 property. And, although 4 percent is a modest annual rate of appreciation compared with what could have been expected a decade ago, in some places and for some kinds of real estate, appreciation could be zero or negative. If your property depreciates and you have to sell and you can't get what you paid for it, guess who will be liable if the ultimate sale price doesn't cover the outstanding balance on the mortgage—the "other people's money" that you rented? Another disadvantage is that real estate is not a liquid investment, which is a major drawback when you need to cash in and get out.

But for most of us who are concerned about recovering and rebuilding our careers and sustaining our recoveries, there's a more serious objection to real estate investing. Like investing in individual stocks, if you do it right it's extremely time-consuming. If you can spare the time and have the aptitude and are seriously considering making real estate investing your second career, then obviously you should pursue the possibilities. But for most people, those who are striving for excellence in their jobs and developing other careers in secondary work, real estate investing is just too time consuming. The development of that second career has to be the first priority.

The other investments described here fit in much better with the lifestyles we now have to adopt. It's better to pay someone else to manage our stock portfolios, which have been increasing in value by 15 percent a year. No leverage here, but, if we're patient, real wealth.

When considering any investment, the basic questions are the important ones:

- Exactly what is the investment? Is that clear to you from the sales literature or prospectus that's been provided to you? If it isn't, and you can't get answers from the investment's sponsor, steer clear.

- What's the track record—how has the investment performed—during the last year, 5, 10, and 15 years? Where can I find out, on a regular basis, how the investment is performing? Can I look in my newspaper's financial section every day, or do I have to call some obscure broker for a quotation?

- How much am I paying, up front, to get into this investment? When does my wealth start to build?

- In the final analysis, the success of your financial recovery depends on defining your objectives in light of your circumstances, and picking and sticking to investments that are compatible with these objectives.

- Your objectives will change as you get older, and so will your investments. They may be different 10 years from now as your careers may have changed. Career planning, financial planning—they fit together and are mutually reinforcing.

CHAPTER SIXTEEN

The Beginning, Not the End

How does it feel? Whether you have actually accepted a job offer, or are generating productive interviews that you know will lead to offers, how does it feel to be in the driver's seat? How does it feel to be in control—far more than you ever thought you could be?

You are entitled to be satisfied with what you've accomplished so far, for you have overcome many formidable obstacles in a world that's getting more competitive every day. And because that world is ever changing, you must continue to change with it. This means that although you can be satisfied, you should not for a minute think you can rest on your laurels.

When you start on a new job, you have come to a beginning, not an ending. With that new beginning must come a determination to comprehend and control the changes that are swirling around you.

Changes such as these:

- The near-certainty of changing jobs at more frequent intervals: voluntary changes, involuntary changes, "anticipatory" changes.

Implications for you: You have to keep your recovery skills honed. Your résumé should be updated twice a year, your network at least that often. When you are not looking you should be trying to help others, living by this version of the Golden Rule: "I'll do all I can for others now, hoping that some may help me when I need it most."

As you get seriously into managing your career and keeping your performance at peak levels, you may even begin critiquing each days' performance on your way home after work. Reviewing the day's game films, so to speak. Not out of guilt or remorse, but for fun, enlightenment, and improvement: "Well, okay, my comments in that sales presentation could have been more responsive. Next time I'll check that while I'm doing it." And, "Darn it, I know that call came in 20 minutes after my normal quitting time, and I don't think I sounded too impatient, but could I have been more helpful? Would I have been more helpful at 9:30 A.M.? Got to watch that. When a customer calls, turn the clock to face the wall."

It is this kind of interest in your work and sensitivity to its requirements that tells you you've found something you enjoy. You're more likely to do well as a result, so that when change does come, it will be you who initiates it. You will think of yourself more and more as an entrepreneur, currently under contract to an employer, rather than as an indentured servant.

- *The unexpected becoming expected:* Nobody can see the future clearly.

Implication for you: It is inevitable that you will be blindsided. You won't be able to avoid that completely. Don't get too uptight when you are affected by change you don't welcome and are not prepared for. No matter what the change is, if you're prepared you'll have more control than ever.

- *Seismic shifts in industries from retailing to banking; re-structuring, reorganizing, downsizing; jobs disappearing permanently.*

Implication for you: You must learn to do more than one type of work at a competitive level of excellence. If you cannot, perhaps you should resign yourself to intermittent bouts of extended unemployment. If you can adapt by becoming multi-talented, you will open a new world of opportunities that never before existed for you.

- *Lifetime employment tenure for fewer people.* Corporate reorganizations have become a permanent part of the landscape. No company that intends to stay competitive will ever again be able to conclude that it has sufficiently downsized its staff.

Implication for you: You may not be able to stay in one place long enough to build up substantial retirement benefits, and you may not want to. You will have to shift a larger percentage of your family expenditures from the present to the future; to invest more, now. You will need the earnings later.

Everyone will see such changes from different perspectives, and everyone will adapt to them differently. Coming up on your screens are two scenarios that illustrate different ways of adapting.

First Scenario: It is six years and two jobs from now. You are two years into a position for which you were recruited after a spectacular four-year run at Lompoc, Limited. You're so good your superiors are embarrassed to give you performance reviews. Not only are you on a fast track, you're on a track by yourself. You're known, liked, and respected companywide and industrywide.

Then, one afternoon in the middle of the week, the COO drops into your office and drops you out: "Richard, your performance here has been flawless; everyone knows that. But unfortunately your performance level is no longer relevant, because, going forward, we're going to get from another department what we've been getting from your group.

"Because of the sensitive nature of your work and the competitive position the company is in, I'll have to ask that you gather your effects and finish up by 5:00 P.M. today. Ms. Hansen from Security will be down to help you pack.

"I want you to know our opinion of you hasn't changed in any way. You will get the highest recommendations. Our corporate legal office has drafted a settlement offer we feel is most reasonable; please get back to us when your attorney has reviewed it. Good-bye and good luck. Oh, of course, I forgot: The outplacement counseling firm of Magnum Ofus will be at your disposal for the next 12 months. Use them as you see fit. Again, good-bye."

You are as stunned as you were the last time something like this happened. You never expected it to happen again. You might be thinking: "So it's back to outplacement counseling, eh, Dick? Nice feeling, isn't it? Is that what you wanted, what you were planning for? Do you think you might have missed something? You picked up a lot along the way: lots of dollars, homes, cars, frequent flier miles. But now at least, you have one-on-one outplacement counseling. No group sessions for you; you're above that level. And they're going to market you! With all that going for you, you're sure to find something. Always have, always will." Even without the bitterness, you are in fact better off than you have been. But perhaps, just maybe, might you wish now that you had done things a little differently? Consider the following situation.

Second Scenario: Twelve years down the road, and you're on your second or third job in your recovery. There are a few clouds on your horizon but they aren't yet particularly dark and they haven't moved in close. What you're doing today, you could not have imagined you'd be engaged in 12 years ago; it has been a rapid upward evolution. And right now you are focusing on the next turn.

You look up from the proposal you've been reading at the kitchen table and share your thoughts with your husband. "John, I think this will get us where we've wanted to go. Full-time consulting for both of us; me, starting soon, you easing into full-time work over the next two years. I think we can hack it; let's be sure."

You adjourn to your personal computer and punch up your financial spreadsheets. As you scroll the numbers past, your conclusions are the same: "One more year of mortgage payments, no other long-term debt. Other assets: various investments, all geared to growth. We've had our ups and downs with these, but the 'ups' have been great. If we reallocate them in this way and take the income we'll get from them, add that to our 'worst-case' estimate of income from consulting, minus 15 percent to be safe, where do we come out? Close enough to do it, it looks like.

"Any second thoughts? Sure: About the nice people we'll be leaving and the nice comfortable situations we'll be giving up. But let's look ahead. We understand what's out there: pressure and competition. Hard work; lots of homework. Nothing different from what we have now, but there is one big difference: we'll have more control now. We can turn the pressure up or down. We can maintain the pace or ease off. All those expenditures we didn't make a dozen years ago have now become cows we can milk for the extra cash we may need. And nobody's going to put us out to pasture when we turn 60 or 70; if we stay current we can do this for years to come. It's not a hard choice to make; we're going ahead."

Two different perspectives, two different sets of choices. Choices are going to be made. The only question is, will you make them or will someone else make them for you?

Obsession + aptitude + enjoyment = excellence
Excellence + tenacity = success
Success + planning = more choices, greater freedom, greater control

Equations to live by.

Index